WHAT DO I DO WHEN
TEENAGERS
QUESTION THEIR
SEXUALITY?

Dr. Steven Gerali

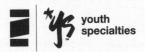

youth
specialties

ZONDERVAN

What Do I Do When Teenagers Question Their Sexuality?
Copyright © 2010 by Steven Gerali

YS Youth Specialties is a trademark of YOUTHWORKS!, INCORPORATED and is registered
with the United States Patent and Trademark Office.

Requests for information should be addressed to:

Zondervan, 3900 Sparks Dr. SE, Grand Rapids, Michigan 49546

ISBN 978-0-310-29198-5

Cover design: Invisible Creature
Interior design: Brandi Etheredge Design

Printed in the United States of America

14 15 16 17 18 19 20 /DCI/ 22 21 20 19 18 17 16 15 14 13 12 11 10 9 8 7 6 5 4 3

Contents

What Do I Do When...
BOOK SERIES
| INTRODUCTION |
Read This First!

It's very important you read this Introduction. This series of books has grown out of years of listening to professional and volunteer youth workers wrestle through difficult ministry situations. I usually know what's coming when the conversation starts with, "What do I do when...?" Most of the time they're looking for remedial help, but many times the issues covered in this book series have no preventive measures available. Many of these issues aren't given serious thought until they evidence themselves in the fabric of ministry. Then youth workers, church staff, parents, and even teenagers scramble to get some kind of understanding, remedy, support, or theological perspective on the situation. This series is designed to help you.

Before we move too far ahead, you need to know a few things. First, just because you read these books and acquire some helping skills, that doesn't make you a professional counselor or caregiver. In many situations you'll need to help parents and teenagers network with professional mental health workers, medical professionals, or, in some cases, legal counsel. Often the quality of care regarding these issues lies in the rapid response of helping professionals. So if you don't get anything else out of this series, get this:

The best thing you can do as an effective helper is realize you're not a trained counselor and you must refer, refer, refer.

Second, often when youth workers are in the throes of an issue, they'll quickly access the Internet for help and information. Researching something online can be very time-consuming, and it can provide unreliable information. So this book series is designed to offer reliable information that's quickly accessible for anyone who's working with adolescents.

Third, each book follows a similar format designed to help you navigate the information more easily. But more importantly, it also provides a model to help you deal with the issue at hand. What Do I Do When... books are divided into the following four sections:

SECTION 1: UNDERSTANDING THE ISSUE, OR "PRESENTING PROBLEM"

Each book will start with an *epistemology* of the issue—in other words, the knowledge regarding its nature and scope. Many youth workers formulate their opinions, beliefs, and ideas using faulty information that's been passed through the grapevine—often without realizing the grapevine has root rot. Faulty information can change the trajectory of our actions in such a way it actually causes us to miss the mark. And many times our "misses" can be destructive to a kid who's already struggling with a painful issue.

We cannot expect to lead a teenager to the truth of Scripture if we start with a foundation that's built upon a lie or deception. We must be informed, seeking to understand the presenting problem as learners with a teachable spirit. In some cases these books may provide only the basics about an issue. But hopefully they'll be enough to create a solid foundation that gives direction for further research from reliable sources.

SECTION 2: UNDERSTANDING HOW YOUR THEOLOGY INTERSECTS THE ISSUE OR PRESENTING PROBLEM

Each book will also cover at least one theological perspective that informs the situation. However, please note I plan to give theological insights from multiple perspectives, so you'll know the theological voices adolescents and their families hear. Some of these voices may not resonate with your particular view, but it's important you develop a gracious, loving, and understanding heart. Keep in mind you're dealing with desperate, hurting, and broken people who—in the midst of their pain and struggle—are seeking grace and hope, not someone with theological answers.

I realize there's a danger in writing like this. Whenever the playing field is leveled—in other words, when one's internalized theological framework is challenged or an opposing theological view is given—it can quickly become a fisticuffs arena to champion truth. I believe that truth brings freedom (John 8:32). But let's remember that the Pharisees believed they'd cornered the market on truth simply because they held to a rigid interpretation of the Scriptures, yet they failed to listen for God's voice in others—especially in the Messiah.

A dear friend of mine once confronted a group of students by asking, "Is your interpretation of Scripture always right?" The students knew that if they replied affirmatively, then they'd set themselves up as the source of infallibility. So they replied, "No, nobody can be right all the time."

My friend then asked, "In what areas are you wrong?"

His wisdom during that loving confrontation helped those students see that unless they openly and graciously engaged the theological perspectives of others, they'd never know if their own perspectives were lacking. Our goal in helping kids through difficult issues is to usher Christ into their situations. Many times that may not be with answers but with presence, affection, support, and understanding.

I recall a situation in which my dear, sweet, Italian mother was hurting for a young couple who'd been caught in sexual sin (she and my dad had mentored this couple). The disciplinary actions of the church were harsh and shaming. So while the church acted in rightness, it failed to see other theological perspectives that informed this situation, such as a theology of reconciliation, grace, confession, and absolution. In my conversation with my mother, I heard her engage these things because she, too, entered into the process and pain of this young couple, and she refused to apply a static template of dealing with the issue in a "right way." Instead, she decided to deal with the issue first in a loving and good way.

It's important to remember that many times rightness is not goodness. God has called his people to be good (Matthew 5:16, Ephesians 2:10, 1 Timothy 6:17-19)—not always "right." That doesn't mean we ignore truth, nor does it mean we minimize the authority of Scripture. It just means we must be incredibly and painfully careful to err on the side of that which is loving and good. Wrestling through various theological viewpoints, even if we don't initially agree with them, will keep us in the tension of being loving and good.

SECTION 3: CONSIDERING WHAT ACTIONS WE CAN TAKE

When we understand an issue or problem, we must wrestle through the theological and consider appropriate action. That can mean anything from doing more research to aggressively seeking solutions. In this third section, I'll attempt to provide you with a framework for action, including practical examples, applications, and tips. This will only be a skeletal plan you'll need to own and tweak to fit the uniqueness of your situation. There is rarely one prescribed action for an issue—every situation is unique because of the people involved.

Throughout the years, I've watched youth workers attempt to use books about youth ministry as one uses an instruction manual for the assembly of a bicycle. They assume that if they put this screw into this hole, then this part will operate correctly. Likewise, they expect that applying a tip from a book will fix a student or situation. If only life were this easy!

Every example provided in this series of books grows out of my years of ministry and clinical experience, input from God's people, and proven results. But they're not foolproof solutions. God desires to be intimately involved in the lives of students and their families, as they trust in God through their difficult times. There is no fix-all formula—just faithfulness. So as you follow some of the directives or action steps in these books, remember you must prayerfully seek God in the resolution of the issues.

SECTION 4: ADDITIONAL RESOURCES

In this section I'll provide some reliable resources for further help. These Internet sites, books, and organizations can assist you in mobilizing help for teenagers and their families. Hopefully this will save you many hours of hunting, so you can better invest in your students and their families.

Where needed, I'll also give a brief comment or description for the source. For example, some sources will serve to explain a different theological perspective from mainstream. This will help you to be informed before you run out and buy the book or engage the Web site.

I trust this book series will assist you in the critical care of teenagers and their families. God has put you on the front lines of attending, shepherding, and training people who are very dear and valuable to his heart. The way you respond to each person who's involved in these critical issues may have eternal consequences. My prayer is that everyone who reads these books will be empowered in a new way to usher Jesus more deeply and practically into the lives of precious teenagers.

Understanding Sexual Orientation

| Section 1 |

The Wednesday night youth group following the high school winter retreat was supposed to be a recap of the great things God had done over the weekend. The retreat had been so encouraging to Pastor Scott—it felt like just the spiritual boost the youth group had needed. Scott was prepared to show a video recap of the fun they'd all had; he'd asked a number of students to share about their renewed commitments to Christ as well.

About 30 minutes before youth group was to begin, Scott was finalizing things in his office when Kyle, a high school senior and student ministry leader, knocked on his door. He looked concerned. "Can I talk to you about something?" Kyle asked from the doorway.

Pastor Scott invited Kyle to step inside his office, and Kyle sat in the chair across the desk.

"What's going on?" Scott asked.

"Well, I have to talk to you about the retreat—something happened that you need to know about. I haven't told anyone, but I'm really bothered by it," Kyle stated.

Scott shut his office door and encouraged Kyle to continue. Kyle spoke hesitantly: "On Saturday night of the retreat, I woke up around 3 a.m. to use the restroom. It was on the opposite side of the cabin from my bunk, so I tried to be really quiet as I walked over there. It seemed like all the other guys were sleeping, but when I got close to the restroom door, I noticed two guys were in one bunk. And as I got closer...I saw they were kissing each other, and they weren't wearing much clothing."

Kyle went on to tell Scott that he recognized both of the guys. One was a junior whose family was very active in the church. The other was a friend the first guy had brought along on the retreat—a sophomore who'd just started attending youth group.

"They know I saw them," Kyle said. "I went into the restroom; and when I came back, they were in their own bunks pretending to be asleep."

The youth group meeting was about to start. Scott assured Kyle he'd handle the matter and asked him not to spread the story around. Then he told Kyle he'd get back to him after he figured out what needed to be done.

After Kyle left the office, Scott reached for the Bible on his desk and then paused for a moment. He took a deep breath and said, "Lord, what do I do now?"

1.1 SCOPE OF THIS ISSUE

Homosexuality is one of the foremost issues facing youth ministry today. Youth workers all over the globe have witnessed students openly announce to the rest of the youth group that they're gay. During a series on love, sex, and dating, one girl, who'd been coming to church for only six months, told her youth group she was a lesbian. She assumed her experience wasn't controversial as she tried to explain how Christian principles for dating also informed her relationships.

Another youth pastor felt trapped when his best friend, who was serving as a volunteer in the youth ministry, confessed he was struggling with homosexual thoughts and desires. Most churches' immediate response would be to remove this friend from the ministry. With that being the norm, the youth worker didn't know what to do. If he told his supervisor he'd betray the confessional confidentiality of his friend. He also didn't know how church leadership would respond.

So what do you do when you encounter homosexuality in your church? You may have read these scenarios and immediately thought of a simple solution. If you did, then you may not be aware of the complexity of this issue and the immediate and eternal repercussions of your responses. Alternative sexual lifestyles and the ideologies that accompany them are becoming part of the fabric of our society. Today, media introduce homosexual themes, relationships, and lifestyles as being commonplace. Students are challenged to engage in homosexual activity so they can present themselves as "well-rounded" sexual partners and also learn if they enjoy the experience. Many Universities have gender neutral housing which allows a male and female(one of whom may be gay) to live in the same room or on a gender neutralfloor that shares the same bathroom facilities.

It isn't difficult to find people with strong views about homo-sexuality. There seem to be two militant, polarized views that mark the ideological spectrum. On one side there are many homosexual men and women who believe they're pioneers, suf-fering the scars of an uphill climb to change the antiquated, hateful views of society. Any opposition to their views is labeled as homophobia, a violation of civil rights, or discriminating hate. These voices are passionate and emotional about their cause. Some of them believe they have biblical support for their views and that their opponents take Scripture out of context or read more into it than what's actually there.

On the other side of the spectrum, we find people who believe they're the last bastions in the fight for moral decency; there-fore, they must actively oppose homosexuality on all fronts. They protest at rallies against legislation supporting same-sex mar-riages; many voice their disgust and disdain for homosexuality in any context with the hope of cleansing a corrupt society; and some of the more extreme members carry a perceived pro-phetic message of "God hates Fags" and "Fags go to hell." Any opposition to their view is labeled godless, heretical, or an act of religious persecution against someone taking a stand for biblical truth. These voices are just as passionate and emotional about their stance as the other group. And, not surprisingly, they also believe they have biblical support for their views and that their opponents take Scripture out of context or read more into it than what's actually there.

Both perspectives believe that convincing people to adopt their views will bring freedom and healing. Both groups view any-one with a middle-of-the-road perspective as compromising the truth. And for both sides homosexuality becomes an issue of "rightness." This polarization puts teens in an incredibly difficult place; especially teens who struggle with homosexual urges, have gay friends, or wrestle with an understanding of homosexuality.

The thought of a "middle" perspective on the issue of homosexuality may raise some red flags for you—especially if you see the issue as being black-and-white. You may wonder if I'm going to invite you into a state of neutrality without conviction. I'm not. But I *am* going to ask you to keep reading with an open heart and mind.

Teenagers throughout the world struggle to find answers regarding homosexuality. This struggle takes many forms:

- Teens are already working to formulate their sexual identity. Feelings of same-sex urges and attractions can add more uncertainty to the process.
- Teens are bombarded with the message that you cannot be gay or struggling with homosexual urges and still be a Christian. So Christian teens who are gay feel unwelcome in the church. This rejection perpetuates a crisis of faith and belief as teens feel as though God also rejects them. And gay non-Christian teens also experience rejection by churches and youth ministries when they attend.
- Teens, both gay and straight, struggle to see the church as a place to help them resolve their confusion and formulate their convictions regarding homosexuality. They see the church's convictions and practices in conflict with each other. They may notice the same thing within the gay community. Both groups claim to be embracing communities, but they fail to embrace a person who has different beliefs or who questions the community's convictions.

- Christian teens who believe that homosexuality is wrong live in the tension of how they should respond to gay friends and still be faithful to their convictions.
- Openly gay teens also live with the tension of how they should respond to Christian friends who may oppose their convictions.
- Some teenagers face issues with parents who've come out. This complex situation is multilayered and can be incredibly painful for teens.

In order to get an accurate read, I thought it would be good to have firsthand accounts and actual student voices inform this book. So I contacted 230 youth workers and asked if they could put me in contact with students who were wrestling with homosexuality in some way. The response surprised me; stories poured in from all across the United States, Canada, the United Kingdom, South Africa, Japan, and Australia. Throughout the book you'll see quotations from these students. Names and locations have been changed to protect anonymity, but the words are entirely from teens.

1.1A THE STARTING POINT

This section is critical to understanding the intent of the book and equipping you to effectively help hurting teens who are struggling with their sexuality. As difficult as it may be, the starting point must begin with care for the students—not your theological or ideological view of homosexuality.

Many believe the starting place with struggling teens is to persuade them to embrace their convictions. Those who believe homosexuality is immoral would say they're offering teens freedom from the bondage of sin. Those who are pro-gay would claim they're offering young people freedom from a cultural homophobic stigma and assisting them in discovering their true identity. Both sides would claim they're separating the issue from the teen and the teen from the issue. This is the "love the sinner—hate the sin" theory.

Yet, often both sides will embrace a teen only if he or she agrees with their convictions. If a teenager shows support for an opposing viewpoint, then that teen is written off. Christians may label the adolescent as "lost"; homosexuals might label the teen as "post-gay," "yestergay," "hasbian," or "homophobic." It seems the intention of both perspectives is about being right in their convictions and is never really about the teen.

When we lead by presenting our stance on an issue, we show little regard for the person and the struggles he or she is experiencing. We must fight the urge to lead from our theological or ideological views and instead create a safe place where teens are loved and valued.

"I think both the gay community and the church are trying to help...both are trying to convert teens to what they see as being right, true, and even biblical." — Sarah, a 24-year-old graduate student and lesbian who serves with gay teenage groups in Georgia

Should our convictions ever guide our actions? I can hear some readers saying, "You can't live without convictions, nor should you compromise your convictions." I'd agree with that, although I'd also say that your convictions should be in subjection to the Holy Spirit and the Bible (which we'll address more in just a bit).

I'm not asking people to abandon their convictions or embrace or accept someone else's convictions. I'm simply saying that conviction isn't the starting point if you desire to help a teenager who's struggling with sexuality.

The starting place should always be to value the *person* more than you value your own convictions. Valuing the person is the *good* thing that takes precedence over the *right* thing, as your convictions deem it.

Over and over Jesus calls us to be GOOD, not RIGHT (Matthew 5:16; 7:17-19; 12:33-37; 25:21; Luke 3:8-9; 6:27, 33-36). Later, the apostle Paul teaches us that we're created for good works (Ephesians 2:10) and that among the fruits of the Holy Spirit that should be evidenced in a believer's life is goodness (Galatians 5:22). You'll notice that holding on to correct doctrine is not on that list. Evangelical Christians have become so concerned about compromising their theology that they'll wage a war just to make sure that everyone knows their position regarding homosexuality. There's a time and place to take a theological stand, but it seems the banner we unfold is not a Christ banner but a position banner. This makes the church a very unsafe place where students must navigate treacherous waters in isolation. It's far better for us to be known by our love, mercy, grace, and goodness than by our theological position on homosexuality.

Your views about this issue will inform the way you guide and counsel students; but it shouldn't affect the way you view them or the quality of your care for them. With that in mind, you must be open-minded as you come to a fuller understanding of what students will hear, encounter, learn, feel, and struggle through.

If you hold fast to voicing your convictions, you'll never know the teens' painful journeys. You'll never do ministry in a relational, incarnational way.

Incarnational ministry follows Jesus' example of "becoming like" (John 1:14). God became like us by taking on human flesh. We become like teens by knowing more about them and the world in which they journey than they do. If we're really honest, most of us would say we're drawn to ministry with young people who are like us—not marginalized kids. Nevertheless, if we're going to work with today's adolescents (ages 12 to 23), then we'd better become more knowledgeable, understanding, and equipped to deal with homosexuality.

Hopefully this book will give you a broader understanding of the issue of homosexuality and those dealing with it. Teenagers who struggle with homosexuality have probably searched out more theology, theories, culture, and voices that will help them than you have. The person who is the most understanding, loving, nonjudgmental, gracious, and safe is the person who's able to walk with a student through this tough issue.

Without question, the issue of homosexuality divides churches. There are many who believe homosexuality is acceptable in some form or variation, while others believe it's sin in every form. By asking the reader to be open-minded, I realize I've made myself a target. However, I've done my best to write this book in an unbiased manner. While it isn't possible to be entirely impartial, I hope I'll at least keep you guessing as to where I personally stand on this issue. And I do this to serve as an example of incarnational ministry. I want you to read the views, theologies, theories, and advice your teenagers will hear. I want you to mentally walk through their processes. I want you to learn to be quick to listen and slow to speak. I want you to be more compassionate than you were before.

The starting place is to be a learner who's passionate about students and will walk alongside them through life's journeys. This perspective will make you *and* the church a safer place for struggling teens.

Having said that, you must understand that **this book is NOT a primer or treatise on homosexuality, nor is it meant to be a comprehensive work.** That means that theories and theologies will be presented (all of which have vague interpretations) without qualification. They'll just be represented as part of what teenagers will encounter. You won't find arguments or rebuttals here. You won't be told what to think or not to think. It's my opinion that you need to research your own theology on this issue. Youth workers must put themselves in subjection to the Holy Spirit's teaching and guidance. The Spirit convicts and formulates conviction.

"I've struggled with homosexual thoughts since my teenage years. I believe homosexuality is sin, and I'd never want people to know my struggle. It seems like churches are gracious about most everything but this issue. I can't share about this... even if I'm experiencing victory over it. People are too scared and condescending in the church. If I share that I've struggled some, I might lose my job." — Mark, a 23-year-old youth pastor from Illinois

I have a dear colleague who'd often ask people in ministry, "Are your theologies always right?" The obvious and humble answer is no. He'd then ask, "Which ones are the wrong ones?" In his wise way, he made others come to understand that we never know if we're wrong in our understanding of Scripture and theology unless we put ourselves in humble submission to the Holy Spirit's teaching. He is God, the Helper who invades our hearts and minds, renewing them constantly.

This book is about helping teenagers whose lives have been put into turmoil over homosexuality.

"I told my best friend in our youth group that I thought I might be gay. We've been friends and going to the same church since I was three. I thought I could trust him not to tell anyone. But he said he believed the right thing to do was to tell. So I got confronted by the youth leaders, and they told my parents, and it leaked out to people all over the church. It hurts. I feel betrayed and humiliated." — Randy, an 18-year-old senior in Idaho

1.1B HAVING A PROPER ATTITUDE
Homosexuality is an emotion-packed issue. People have felt the pain of rejection, lost their hopes and dreams, and felt an overwhelming fear of judgment because of it. It's torn apart families, destroyed lives, and brought incredible persecution and even death to many people. The emotional and personal dynamics of this issue should cause us to be gracious in our approach.

I believe a proper attitude is required. If we want to effectively help teenagers who are wrestling through the issue of homo-sexuality, then our attitude must be shaped by the following four factors:

1. Humility: We're invited by the apostle Paul to have the same attitude that was found in Christ. In Philippians 2:1-11, Paul describes this attitude as regarding others as more important than you: "Do nothing out of selfish ambition or vain conceit. Rather, in humility value others above yourselves, not looking to your own interests but each of you to the interests of the others" (vv. 3-4). Jesus demonstrated this by emptying himself and dying for sinful people. This attitude of high positive regard for others is the first factor that must shape our attitude whenever we encounter people who are gay or working through their convictions about homosexuality.

I recently went to lunch with a friend, and we began talking about this book. He commented, "Homosexuality is the issue in the church that makes us feel good about ourselves." When I asked him what he meant, he said, "We make this the queen mother of all sin. It's like the Pharisee in the temple who prayed aloud and thanked God that he wasn't like those sinners. That Pharisee didn't think he was without sin; he just saw everyone else's sin as greater than his own. He saw others as less impor-tant. But Jesus said, 'All those who exalt themselves will be humbled, and those who humble themselves will be exalted.'" (See Luke 18:9-14.)

2. Love: The most identifiable mark that a person is a true Christ-follower is that he or she is loving. The first and con-tinuous attitude should be saturated with love. We often forget this is the primary command on the Christian life. Jesus makes it a mandate, noting that the entire Law and writings of the prophets can be summarized down to loving God and loving

others (Matthew 22:34-40). Jesus later tells his disciples in his final discourse that the one command he leaves them is that they must love one another (John 13:34).

When we're in the heat of this issue of homosexuality, too often we forget that we're to be defined first and foremost by our love. We so passionately want to make our ideas heard and stand for what is right that we forget to act in a loving, kind, and gracious way. We need to remember Paul's words: "If I speak in human or angelic tongues, but do not have love, I am only a resounding gong or a clanging cymbal. If I have the gift of prophecy and can fathom all mysteries and all knowledge, and if I have a faith that can move mountains, but do not have love, I am nothing" (1 Corinthians 13:1-2).

3. Goodness: Christians are also to be marked by goodness, which produces actions, behaviors, and works that are good. We're quick to call out sin and take our stand against issues without thinking about whether the repercussions of our right actions yield goodness. I've heard so many church leaders say time and again, "We had the right thing in mind, but we went about it the wrong way." If only they'd get into the practice of asking themselves if what they're about to do is *good*. Good works are generated from a strong character that's defined by goodness.

4. Nonjudgmental: I've never met a person who claimed to be judgmental. We all believe we suspend judgment and condemnation, yet we've all heard someone say to us, "Don't judge me." It's very difficult to see that we may be judgmental and condemning even when we believe we're doing the right thing. Again, we see this effect revealed in Scripture.

A group of well-meaning men catch a woman in sexual sin. They're passionate about staying true to the Scriptures and demand that the right action be taken. Culturally, that means the woman should be stoned for her immoral behavior. These religious leaders stand in the position of rightness, upholding the truth of the Scriptures. And because of that stance, they don't see themselves as being judgmental. So Jesus helps them to see just how awful their judgmental attitudes are by saying, "Let any one of you who is without sin be the first to throw a stone at her" (John 8:7). The only way we can be nonjudgmental is to see our own sins and limitations.

On another occasion Jesus taught that a no-judgment attitude is the best. He said, "Be merciful, just as your Father is merciful. Do not judge, and you will not be judged. Do not condemn, and you will not be condemned. Forgive, and you will be forgiven" (Luke 6:36-37). I don't want to be judged, humiliated, persecuted, alienated, or condemned—so I won't do those things to someone else. However, I do want to be treated mercifully if I'm in error, and I do want to receive forgiveness if I sin. Therefore, I need to be merciful and forgiving.

1.2 WHAT IS HOMOSEXUALITY?

Sexuality can mean erotic desires, responses, and urges; it can refer to a person's identity; it can define a pattern of thinking and life view. Sexuality is a lens through which we see relationship, family, attraction, romance, and gender.

The word *homosexual* engulfs all the descriptions of sexuality listed above, but it's directed toward someone of the same gender. The word is derived from the Greek *homo* (meaning "same") and *sexual* (the word we use to encompass anything related to sexuality). *Homosexuality* can be defined as "a predominance of cognitive, emotional, and sexual attractions primarily or exclusively to those of the same gender."

Identifying someone as gay is difficult. The baggage, myths, and ignorance we have regarding sexuality—let alone homosexuality—minimize the complexity of the issue. Labeling a behavior, person, attitude, or ideology "gay" can be dangerous and misdirected. For example, a feminine-acting male or a masculine-acting female may not be gay. As we try to understand heterosexuality and homosexuality, we must be sensitive and agree that labels should never be universally applied. Some would identify a person as a homosexual only if he or she engages in homosexual behaviors. This would mean that sexual urges and desires don't necessarily mean someone is gay; it's engaging in the behavior that brings definition.

"When I was 13, someone spoke to my youth group about masturbation. They made a side comment that if a guy likes touching that part of himself that much, then something must be wrong with him. I was terrified by this. I tried to stop masturbating, but I kept getting drawn back to it. This made me think I must be gay. I was thinking about girls sexually, and I knew I wasn't supposed to do that either, so this was really confusing."
— Mike, a 17-year-old senior from Wisconsin

Some hold to an opposite view, believing that same-gender sexual attraction, desires, and urges define a person as gay. According to this view, there are many gay Christians who remain celibate—admitting they're gay but not acting on their feelings. This is equated to someone who identifies herself as an alcoholic but doesn't indulge in her desires for a drink.

Others may say that a homosexual is one who experiences attraction, sexual urges, and drive, and may also engage in sexual behaviors (flirting, dating, physical contact, and so on) with someone of the same gender. This is by far the most widely held understanding of who a homosexual is.

Still others may say that being a homosexual involves attraction, sexual behavior, and identifying oneself as homosexual.

"I recently told my friends and family back home that I'm gay. I decided not to tell my friends at school. I want the people around me to define me as a Christian man...not just a gay man." — David, a 19-year-old sophomore at a Christian university

Merton P. Strommen, in his book *The Church and Homosexuality: Searching for a Middle Ground*, observed six different classifications of homosexuals:

1. Devout Homosexuals: Gay individuals who are committed to Christ and the church. The majority believe homosexuality is a sin, so they remain celibate in order to honor moral boundaries. Some of these men and women may never come out to anyone about their homosexuality. Others in this camp deviate slightly, believing the moral boundary can include a same-gender, committed, monogamous relationship. By far these gay Christians believe they're defined by more than their sexual orientation.

2. Non-churched, Discreet Gays: These gay men and women seek to live quietly with a partner. Many are in professions that mandate they be discreet (doctors, politicians, teachers, lawyers, and so on). While they contribute to the social good, they remain uninvolved in gay social activism.

3. Militant Gays or Gay Social Activists: These are people who live an openly gay lifestyle and use it as a statement of social activism. Their desire is to see a gay lifestyle and worldview embraced as a normal alternative. Gay activists may see themselves as the vocal majority for the homosexual community as they actively seek to change legislation on same-sex marriage; work to see homosexuality presented in both the media and educational institutions as a positive and acceptable alternative lifestyle; seek the ordination of gay clergy; and lobby for adoption rights for same-gender parents. Gay activists often encourage all homosexuals to be "fully out," which means they accept an openly gay lifestyle (including all the above causes).

4. Closeted Gays: These are people living with a sense of guilt and shame over their homosexuality. They may be seeking ways to change their sexual orientation, while living with a great deal of anxiety and confusion. They also live in fear of being "outed."

5. Promiscuous Gays: These are gay men and women (more often men) who believe the only expression of homosexuality is sexual. They don't seek relationships; they only seek sex. Many gay and lesbian people are frustrated by those living a promiscuous gay lifestyle because they create such negative public attention. Some promiscuous gays have fought public decency laws because they feel such laws violate their freedoms of expression.

6. Homosexual Subcultures: These are gay men and women who engage in fetishes and paraphilia in their lifestyle and sexuality.

An example of this would be the leather subculture, which venerates bondage, domination, sadism, and masochistic sexual rituals and games. Other subcultures include mature men partnered with younger men. But it doesn't mean men having sex with kids; the subculture is built on role-play between men with a 10-year or more age difference (for example, a 30-year-old with a 50-year-old). This "Dads and Lads" subculture includes sexual role-play surrounding any event or relationship in which an older man encounters a younger man (e.g., an athlete and coach, a father and son, and so on). Some question whether this arrangement could become a trap for young, questioning teens. It's important to know that MOST of the people who are a part of this subculture are NOT pedophiles, and they make sure their younger partner is of legal age. However, it's true that pedophiles will use avenues like this subculture to lure teens. A gay teen may initiate a relationship while lying about his age in order to gain sexual attention and experience from an older male (for instance, a 16-year-old with a 22-year-old). The Internet is the most common venue for initiating these types of hookups.

1.3 UNDERSTANDING HOMOSEXUAL CULTURE

If we want to make our youth ministries safe places where teens can talk about their struggles, it's important for us to understand some of the issues and terminology surrounding homosexuality. Many teens who wrestle with homosexuality are familiar with and may even use some of the terms listed in this section.

The following list is comprised of terms, slang words, and cultural markers that directly intersect adolescence. I've encountered many youth workers who didn't know some of these terms or had a totally different understanding of them. You may find some of the terms and descriptions offensive. I hope you'll be able to get past this. My desire is that these terms will help you to be more informed and able to engage in healthy dialogue about the issues relating to homosexuality. In addition, I hope you won't view this section as just a glossary of terms. Your understanding of a term may shift as you encounter some of the definitions presented here.

1.3A COMMON TERMS

AIDS (Acquired Immune Deficiency Syndrome): The long-term effect of the Human Immunodeficiency Virus (HIV). AIDS alters the proper functioning of the human immune system, rendering it helpless against all viruses and cancer. There is no known cure for HIV/AIDS, although medical advancements have been made in slowing the progression of the virus. Some Christians have made bold statements about how this disease is God's judgment on the homosexual community. (Even more people believe this is true.) Yet the virus isn't restricted to just homosexuals. It's passed on from the exchange of bodily fluids, including the transmission from mother to child in utero or through breast-feeding.

Alternative Sexual Lifestyle: This is a phrase that was first used a few decades ago, for a man or woman engaged in a lifestyle of homosexuality. It has become the politically correct way to identify a homosexual culture as an alternative to the heterosexual norm.

Bi-curious: See **Gay-curious.**

Bisexuality: This is the term used for people who define their sexual orientation as neither heterosexual nor homosexual. It's a misconception to believe that these people are sexually confused, sexual addicts, sexually whoring, nymphomaniacs, or have a hyperactive sexual desire disorder. They define their sexual drives and desires toward both genders as equal. Bisexuality can fall on a continuum between heterosexuality and homosexuality. Some bisexuals claim to have

- A homosexual orientation prior to exclusive heterosexual orientation or vice versa
- Predominant homosexual orientation with infrequent heterosexual contacts or vice versa
- Equal orientation and contacts toward members of both sexes
- Equal orientation toward members of both sexes followed by exclusive contacts or relationships (also referred to as **Sequential Bisexuality**)

Butch: A label given to a gay man or woman who epitomizes a masculine stereotype in dress, behavior, and attitude.

Closeted (or **Not Out**): A person who has sexual attractions for a member of the same gender but never acknowledges them—either personally (creating an inner conflict or, some would believe, a state of personal denial) or to others. Some closeted men and women may be active in the homosexual community but keep their homosexuality hidden in the rest of their life routines.

Cross Dresser (or **Transvestite**): A person who becomes sexually aroused by not only wearing the clothing, but also taking on the traits, behaviors, and identity of the opposite gender. Often a cross dresser is not a gay person. Homosexual transvestites are usually referred to as **drag queens** (males who impersonate females) or **drag kings** (females who impersonate males).

Cut: A circumcised male. If he is uncircumcised, then he's referred to as **uncut**.

Dads and Lads: A homosexual subculture that's characterized by relationships between mature men and younger adult men with a 10-year or more age difference (for example, a 30-year-old with a 50-year-old). This subculture includes sexual role-play surrounding any event or relationship in which an older man would encounter a younger man (e.g., an athlete and coach, a father and son, and so on).

Dyke: A demeaning and derogatory label for a gay, bisexual, or transgendered female.

Down Low (or **DL**): The term used when a man discreetly has sex with another man while in another sexual relationship with a woman. The man having sex on the DL doesn't consider himself gay or bisexual. He does it for sheer sexual pleasure without his female partner (wife or girlfriend) being aware of it. There is an increasing belief among college men that DL experiences are part of keeping themselves sexually "well-rounded." This type of relationship is usually considered **NSA** (no strings attached); it's strictly sexual.

Egodystonic Homosexuality: The persistent and marked distress or depression over one's homosexual identity and orientation.

Fag: A demeaning and derogatory label for a gay, bisexual, or transgendered male. It's shortened from the word *faggot*, which was an old-world term given to an unpleasant woman. The slang word became popular in modern times to describe gay men. The word *faggot* also refers to a bundle of wood used to stoke a fire. Some believe there's a connection between this meaning and the modern label, in that homosexuals were burned as heretics.

Femme: Description of a male with effeminate or female traits and mannerisms. Putting this label on a young teen who's working through masculine identity development can have a detrimental effect. Not all guys with feminine characteristics are gay, nor do all gay guys fit a feminine stereotype.

Friend of Dorothy: An undercover term used by the gay community to refer to a man who is gay. Judy Garland, who played Dorothy in *The Wizard of Oz*, is an icon to the gay community. In the film Dorothy's acceptance of those who were outcast and her desire to help them in their plight becomes the tie-in.

Gay: Slang term used to identify someone who's homosexual, either male or female. It's become the culturally accepted term for homosexuality. Originally, it was used to describe someone who was overly happy, carefree, or energetically engaging. But as far back as the seventeenth century, it also had some connotations of sexual frivolity and even immorality. By the mid-twentieth century, the word *gay* was used antithetically to the word *straight*, which meant "socially acceptable." Eventually, the term *gay* became a more acceptable word for "homosexuality" than the popular term *queer* being used at that time.

Gay-curious: A person who wants to explore homosexuality both emotionally and physically. Gay-curious teenagers maybe coming to terms with their own sexuality, or they may just want to have the experience of a same-gender sexual encounter. The term *bi-curious* is often interchanged with this term. The difference between the two is that in the latter, the individual may have a greater attraction to one gender and merely desire to explore any feelings and urges that would label them as bisexual.

Gaydar: A gay person's ability to discern if others are gay or bisexual when they're in a group of heterosexuals. Although some would like to think it's a sixth sense, *gaydar* may just be a keen intuitive read on shared attitudes, values, culture, behaviors, and so on.

Gender Confusion: The process by which an individual identifies more strongly with the opposite gender. Many transsexuals go through this process beginning in early childhood when they start to understand gender. An individual may identify with the opposite gender and believe she's a man trapped in a woman's body or vice versa. (See **transsexual.**)

Gender Identity: The process of identifying oneself as a woman or a man and others appropriately as men or women. Throughout childhood boy and girls learn masculinity and femininity from the behaviors, roles, expectations, norms, and appearances that are ascribed to men and women. Through mimicking, adopting, and later internalizing these gender traits, they learn to be men or women (not just male or female). In adolescence gender identity is a major component of the identity process because (1) adolescents are changing cognitively, meaning they can grasp and internalize the abstract scope and limitations of gender, and (2) their physiology is changing to allow them to experience gender-specific functions and the fullness of all that comes with those changes.

Gender Reassignment: More commonly known as a sex-change procedure, this is the surgical alteration of genitalia and breasts to reassign a male to a female or a female to a male. A person who undergoes this procedure is usually identified as a transsexual, although some people are born with both male and female genitalia (an anomaly known as **hermaphroditism** or **intersexuality**). Intersex persons are usually assigned a gender at the discretion of their parents. Some intersex people suffer with the identity and desires of being assigned and raised as the wrong gender. Many of these individuals don't discover they were gender assigned until they reach puberty and begin experiencing sexual drives and growth.

Gay & Lesbian Alliance Against Defamation (GLAAD): An organization whose mission is to serve as the watchdog over the media's portrayal of homosexuality to ensure it's done in a positive light.

GLBT: The acronym commonly used to identify the community of gay, lesbian, bisexual, and transgendered people. Sometimes the letter I is added to the end to include **intersexual** persons.

Gay, Lesbian and Straight Education Network (GLSEN): A national organization that strives to assure that each member of every school community is valued and respected regardless of sexual orientation or gender identity and expression.

Gay-Straight Alliances (GSA): Student-led clubs in which gay and straight students join together to create safe environments on high school campuses (primarily in the United States). Through these clubs students support each other; learn about homophobia and other oppressions; work together to educate the school community about homophobia, gender identity, and sexual orientation issues; and fight discrimination, harassment, and violence in schools.

Hasbian: The gay community's term for a lesbian who's chosen a heterosexual life. It's the female counterpart of a **Yestergay.**

Homoeroticism: Term used for same-gender sensuality portrayed in media, art, literature, and cinema.

Homo-hop: An alternative genre of the hip-hop culture that embraces homosexual themes, artists, and lifestyles.

Homophile: A person who supports and acts as an advocate for the rights and lifestyle of the homosexual community. One reason parents of homosexual children struggle through the resolution of this issue is that they're often expected to become advocates as a means of showing their love and support.

Homophobia: This term refers to any negative reactions, values, behaviors, and attitudes toward homosexuality and GLBT individuals. It doesn't refer to a fear of homosexuals or homosexuality, although if someone were afraid of becoming a homosexual, then that person would be called homophobic.

Homosexual: The more widely used term for anyone who has a physical, romantic, or emotional attraction to the same gender. This becomes very complex when we add other variables and situations. For example, a person may fantasize about or engage in a same-sex encounter and not be homosexual; yet another individual may never have a homosexual experience but because their sexual desires and drives are same-gender directed, they could be considered a homosexual. This issue is even more complex in teens, who are still forming their sexual identities. They may believe that if they have a strong love attachment to a member of the same gender or if they had an arousing sexual experience with a member of their own gender, then they must be homosexual. This isn't necessarily true. Some guys have been told that if they enjoy masturbation and frequently engage in that act, then they're homosexual. This conclusion is reached from a belief that the enjoyment of touching the male anatomy leads to homosexuality—especially in light of the fact that the messages they receive about being a sexually virile man say they should have women satisfying their sexual needs. In addition, guys fight against internalizing Christian virtues such as love, gentleness, meekness, and so on because they identify those traits and the emotive connectedness they generate as being feminine at best, but homosexual in the broadest scope.

Homosocial: This term is used to describe the strong nonsexual bond between members of the same gender who aren't gay. More commonly referred to as a "sisterhood" or "brotherhood," sororities and fraternities can be identified as homosocial communities. The media has effectively labeled a homosocial male relationship as a **"bromance."** In the context of homosexuality, the term has come to refer to the strong nonsexual bond between a straight and a gay person. Many students are wrestling through this because they've developed close friendships with same-gendered friends who later came out. Most homosocial relationships endure the ridicule of both the gay and straight community.

House: A collective group of GLBT people who've been rejected by their families and find themselves homeless. The house serves as a home, most likely run by gay adults who act as parents and mentors for alienated gay teenagers.

Human Immunodeficiency Virus (HIV): HIV attacks the T cells of the human body's immune system and renders them ineffective. **HIV-2** is a second strain of the virus that progresses more slowly and is milder than HIV. This strain is common in parts of Africa, but not as common in Western cultures.

Lesbian: A gay woman.

Lover (or **Partner**): The term used by a person in a homosexual dyadic relationship when referring to his or her homosexual partner. Since there is no homosexual equivalent for *husband, wife,* or *fiancée,* the word *lover* may be used. In a more committed monogamous relationship, the term *partner* is used. Gay men and women may also refer to a significant other as a "boyfriend" or "girlfriend." While the term *girlfriend* is still widely used by heterosexual women to identify other women in their social circles, gay women tend to use the term *lover* to identify their romantic sexual partners.

Metrosexual: A straight man who adopts the styles, grooming practices, and culture that some believe to be indicative of the gay community. Metrosexual men have no problem with getting manicures, primping, wearing high fashion, and so on.

Out (or **Coming Out**): The process by which a person (most likely during adolescence) identifies, accepts, and discloses his or her same-gender sexual desires and attractions. Being "partially out" means a person may have disclosed his or her homosexuality to select individuals but hasn't made it known to all family members or friends. Some GLBT communities believe a person isn't out until he or she has embraced this sexual identity and lives openly as a gay male or female. Coming out is a painful and scary process for a GLBT teenager. A fear of rejection, ridicule, and even abuse often accompanies the process.

Passing: The protective role a gay teenager takes on in order to be seen as heterosexual. This could include dating, sexual experimentation with the opposite gender, engaging in locker-room talk about sexual virility with the opposite gender, acting out heterosexual life scripts, and avoiding anything that could even remotely label him or her as "gay." Teens learn this behavior as part of gender identity, engaging in those behaviors and later redefining them through the process of coming out. Passing makes life safer in the short term, while it complicates the inner turmoil of a gay teenager who already believes he or she is abnormal. *Passing* is also used to describe a person who leads a double lifestyle—having a homosexual identity to some and a heterosexual identity to others.

Parents, Families & Friends of Lesbians & Gays (PFLAG): An international organization that serves as an advocacy group supporting gay, lesbian, bisexual, and transgendered people and their families. PFLAG's mission also involves educating societies about ill-informed views of homosexuality, championing diversity, ending discrimination, and securing equal rights.

Post-gay: This label is often given to gay men or women who don't associate or align with the mainstream gay culture. Post-gay individuals define themselves by something other than their sexual orientation. They may also choose to be identified as **post-labeled**, refusing to have their sexuality defined as gay, lesbian, or bisexual. Post-labeling ideation has some rootedness in gay and lesbian theologies, which see sexual desire and sexuality as natural in any state and therefore regard labeling to be a form of prejudice and therefore regard labeling of any kind to be a form of prejudice, a creation of sinful mankind and an assault against the goodness of God.

Queen: A male who behaves with, dresses with, and adapts to feminine characteristics.

Queer: In its original meaning, the term meant that something was odd, unusual, or outside the cultural norm. In the mid-20th century, *queer* became an antiquated way of referring to homosexuality. So the word **gay** was adopted. More recently the word *queer* has been resurrected as a term of empowerment, but only when used about and by gay and lesbian people. For example, a bisexual wouldn't call him or herself gay but might use the term *queer*. In many cases it's still offensive for a straight individual to refer to a homosexual as queer. But the gay community can use it, as in the case of Bravo's makeover show *Queer Eye for the Straight Guy*, which aired from 2003 to 2007.

Questioning: The descriptor used to define the process in which an individual engages and experiments with homosexuality to determine if he or she is gay, bisexual, or just desirous of gay sexual encounters. Many students who are wrestling with their sexual identities and feelings may be questioning. Questioning is often the beginning of the coming out process. Once an individual comes to terms with his or her sexuality, that person is no longer questioning.

Reparative Therapy (sometimes called **Reorientation Therapy** or **Conversion Therapy**): A therapeutic intervention method with a goal of converting the client from his or her homosexual orientation to a heterosexual one. It's the work of American psychologist Joseph Nicolosi and others, and it's built on the premise of Freudian theory that says sexual conditioning and later orientation is formulated early in the parent-child relationship. Advocates of conversion therapy believe that any rift in that early conditioning can lead an individual to seek out close, intimate relationships with members of the same gender during puberty and on into adolescence. These intimate feelings later become sexual desires directed toward members of the same gender. Thus, reparative therapy attempts to repair that early rift through reconditioning or converting orientation. This is accomplished through the development of healthy, nonsexual intimate relationships with same-gendered individuals, starting with the therapist and support group members.

Gay individuals who undergo reparative therapy are encouraged to strongly embrace and engage in stereotypical gender roles and scripts in order to develop their sense of masculinity or femininity. Additionally, they're discouraged from engaging in any behavior, role, or script that could traditionally define the opposite gender. Therefore, men are encouraged to embrace the bravado of masculinity and avoid any behaviors that could be viewed as weak or feminine.

At the core of this intervention strategy is the assumption that strong gender re-identification results in a re-imprinted, relearned, or converted heterosexual orientation, thereby reversing the individual's sexual desires. There are many who believe this therapy is harmful, claiming that a person is born with his or her particular sexuality and it shouldn't be tampered with.

Many others claim to have genuinely experienced a conversion of sexual desire through reparative therapy.

Sexual Orientation: The enduring sexual, affective, emotional, and erotic attractions one feels for others. Orientation can range on a continuum from being completely heterosexual to being completely homosexual, with varying degrees of bisexuality in between. Because this range is wide, sexual orientation is determined by an individual's self-assessment and self-identity.

Sexual Reorientation: Therapeutic process in which a gay individual engages to stop being gay and become heterosexual. These programs are sometimes called "ex-gay programs." (See also **Reparative Therapy.**)

Sodomy: Technical term used for the act of anal sexual intercourse. The term has an offensive connotation and is often used to describe a criminal act—forced anal intercourse (indicating that the victim has been sodomized). The term has its roots in the biblical account of Sodom and Gomorrah. A mob of men from Sodom tried to break down Lot's door with the intention of having forced sexual relations with his male guests (Genesis 19). This act of forced sexual aggression became known as sodomy.

Stromo: The opposite of a metrosexual in that the term is used for a gay male who immerses himself in the bravado of the straight male culture.

Survival Sex: Many GLBT teenagers end up living on the streets because they're either kicked out of their homes or leave home because of the abusive environments there. Some teenagers who live on the streets exchange sex with older men for food and a place to sleep for the night, as well as cash and drugs. Both heterosexual and homosexual street kids engage in survival sex out of desperation, but it's more prevalent among GLBT teens.

Transformational Ministry: Pastoral counselors' term for ministries that advocate and practice sexual reorientation or conversion therapies. Exodus International is one of the most notable transformational ministries.

Transgendered: A person who believes that he or she was born a specific gender opposite of their physical anatomy (in other words, a man trapped in a woman's body or a woman trapped in a man's body). Not all homosexuals see themselves as transgendered. Many gay men want to be men who are sexually attracted to men. Gay women are sexually attracted to other women. But transgendered individuals believe they're behaving in a way that's true to their inborn genders, but their bodies are anomalies. From early childhood many have a history of hating their genitalia and naturally exhibiting traits that are more indicative of the opposite gender than what their physiology ascribes. Parents of transgendered individuals often affirm that their son always believed he was a girl or that their daughter always believed she was a boy. Many transgendered individuals seek gender reassignment. This process is often long, painful, and costly. The psychological readjustment, hormone therapy, and social restructuring (all known as **transitioning**) can take years. Additionally, being transgendered is not the same thing as intersex (hermaphroditism) in that the transgendered individual's physiology shows no abnormality.

Transsexual: Individuals who identify themselves as members of the opposite gender contrary to their own physical anatomy. This could include transgendered individuals but isn't restricted to them. Many transsexuals seek sex-change or gender reassignment surgery.

Transvestite: See **Cross Dresser.**

Try-sexual: A new term describing a current culture of adolescents who view sexuality through a lens in which they'll try anything at least once to see if it fits them.

Twink: A young gay male. Some underage gay teenagers are referred to as **tweens.**

Yestergay: The gay community's term for a gay man who's chosen a heterosexual lifestyle. It's the male counterpart of a **Hasbian.**

Drew, a 15-year-old sophomore, emailed his youth pastor this: "I'm gay. People think it's a choice to become gay. But I swear to God if it was, I would have chosen a normal life...If there is a God, why would he do this to me? Someone said that in the Bible gay guys go to hell. Why would God create me just to torture me? That's the story of my life...I hope you can help me."

1.3B CULTURE OF GAY TEENAGERS
Culture can be defined as the complete way of living as it's embraced by a group of people. Culture is evidenced by a collective set of values, biases, norms, language, history, traditions, roles, ideals, and icons. Years ago homosexuality was "in the

closet" and away from public view. Some states even had laws making any homosexual act (even between consenting adults) an illegal offense. But in the last few decades, homosexuality has emerged as a dominant subculture. This raises the question of whether GLBT individuals are growing in number or just becoming more open to mainline culture. It's possible that it may be both.

"I tried to keep my secret contained because I realized that whilst I thought I was gay, I was still only young and so couldn't be sure. And if I came out, it would be very hard to 'go back in,' and then all of the problems and abuse that I experienced would be pointless. Every time I told someone, I'd still use the words, 'I THINK I'm gay.'" — Andrew, a 16-year-old from the United Kingdom

The gay community and human rights activists point to some mile markers that have opened the doors to conversations and even a greater tolerance for homosexuality. The progression has moved from an inhumane intolerance that reduced gay individuals to criminals worthy of death (for the record, this view is still widely held in many countries around the globe) to an emergent tolerance found in many cultures worldwide. Some of those events that chronicle this movement are the following:

- **1939–45:** Hitler's Nazi regime imprisoned and put to death thousands of gay men, women, and teenagers in concentration camps. These people were consigned to wear pink triangles on their clothing to identify them as less than human. During that same decade in the United States, thousands of people were removed from the government and military work force simply because they were suspected of being homosexuals. The U.S. State Department believed they were a threat to the security of the United States. Many outwardly gay individuals were imprisoned or institutionalized following the American Psychological Association's diagnostic criteria that said homosexuality was a dangerous personality disturbance.[1]

• **1969:** Police raided the Stonewall Inn, an undercover gay disco in New York City. This incited a series of violent uprisings later to be known as the Stonewall Riots. This was already an era marked by civil unrest, with groups such as the African American civil rights movement, an anti-war movement, and the women's liberation movement vying against injustice. The Gay Liberation Front (GLF) was established to fight against further discrimination against homosexual people. This movement attracted many late-adolescents and young adults (many of whom were homeless as a result of being alienated from families and friends for their homosexuality) bound by an anti-establishment ideology.[2]

• **June 1970:** The first gay pride marches were organized in commemoration of the Stonewall Riots. These more peaceful demonstrations raised public awareness and advanced the "outing" of homosexuality and the formation of a gay culture.[3]

• **1974:** Both the American Psychiatric Association and American Psychological Association removed homosexuality from their list of mental disorders after groundbreaking research revealed that homosexual men were as emotionally stable and lived lives as productive as heterosexual men.[4]

• **1980s:** The outbreak and spread of HIV/AIDS cast homosexuality in a different light. Many outspoken moralists and conservative Christians touted this as being God's wrath against a perverted sexual abomination. They were humbled slightly when research revealed that heterosexuals also contracted the disease from sexual contact and exchange of body fluids. The devastating and horrific effects of this disease elevated fear and concern within both the gay and heterosexual communities, and groups formed to try to stop the disease from reaching pandemic levels. The rise in private sector, nonprofit institutions as missions of mercy to dying AIDS victims raised awareness in public and governmental organizations to participate in a reconciling, healing rally around this cause.

• **1990s:** Gay pride parades, rallies, and rainbow flags became icons of the homosexual culture.

• **2000:** The arts, entertainment, and media industry began introducing gay themes, issues, and characters. Many daytime soaps introduced gay characters with episodes depicting gay teenagers coming out to their parents (and the turmoil surrounding those events), AIDS, and gay romantic entanglements. Other dramas involving teens followed suit, adding gender identity, sexual orientation, and loss of virginity in a homosexual entanglement as common issues in adolescence. Reality TV, celebrities who've come out, cable television series, and family sitcoms have all advanced homosexuality into the everyday milieu. There are few TV series that haven't introduced a gay theme or character because of the prevalence and profile of this issue among the younger generation. The media has not only raised the awareness of the issue as teenagers encounter it, but also helped to establish and reveal a gay culture.

• **2002:** The U.S. Supreme Court ruled in *Lawrence v. Texas* that "liberty," according to the U.S. Constitution, included private sexual acts between consenting adults, even if they were homosexual.[5] Prior to this, all states had anti-gay laws, many of which were difficult to enforce or were ignored. This ruling set a precedent against anti-gay laws.

- **TODAY:** Gay-friendly businesses and organizations (from bathhouses, bars, gyms, vacation and recreational institutions, and cafés to GLBT student organizations, support groups, and social groups) have become a part of the formation of a gay culture. Technology also contributes to this culture's formation and advancement. Chats, blogs, and online support groups have helped GLBT teens become a part of gay social networks and involved in online relationships. A quick search on any given social network such as Facebook or MySpace collectively will reveal more than 50,000 gay groups.

1.4 THEORIES OF HOMOSEXUALITY AND SEXUAL ORIENTATION

More than ever before, teenagers are asking youth workers, "Why am I gay?" Parents also want answers to this question because they feel overwhelmed when they discover their son or daughter is exploring homosexuality. This single question has prompted researchers, theologians, medical professionals, and scholars to find an answer.

The resulting theories fall under two origin categories:

1. Homosexuality is a product of nature having its origin in creation, genetics, hormones, physiology, and so on.
2. Homosexuality is a product of nurture having its origin in cultural imprinting and encoding, learned behaviors, traumatic experiences, or need deprivation.

Many studies have been conducted and used to support each of these viewpoints. While studies show there is evidence to support both the nature and nurture arguments, **no studies have provided us with conclusive evidence**. Given that we cannot dismiss any theory, nor can we fully say that it's conclusive, we may come to the conclusion that homosexuality is a complex orientation (like heterosexuality) that involves both nature and nurture.

In the next few sections, we'll explore the theories regarding the origin of homosexuality in more detail. It's important for youth workers, parents, and teenagers to have a basic understanding of each of these theories and their pros and cons. This is in no way a comprehensive overview (volumes have been written on each theory), but it's an attempt to whet your appetite to know more. (In the "Resources" section of this book, you'll find a list of written materials that may help you in your continued study.)

1.4A NATURE THEORIES
The nature theory suggests that homosexuals are born that way. Science believes we can determine or find predisposition from genetics. In many cases with diseases, anomalies, and syndromes, we can. But when we're dealing with predispositions toward nonphysical traits (such as character traits, right- or left-handedness, or homosexuality), we can't determine anything conclusive.

There are two theories of origin that grow out of this view of nature:

1. Genetics: Scientists continue to search for a genetic link that could predispose a person to a non-heterosexual orientation. Family histories, twin studies, and a host of other studies have been done. Behavioral geneticists have identified and examined markers on chromosomes in gay men and women, but they haven't found sufficient correlations. At one point researchers believed they'd identified a "gay gene," citing

a link between homosexuality and the Xq28 chromosome segment. This turned out to be crucial enough to merit a connection, but ultimately the finding was inconclusive. Yet many people still use these study results to support a genetic predisposition. Both gay and heterosexual researchers agree there could be some genetic connection, but there's nothing that gives us sufficient evidence to say that homosexuality is genetically determined. On the other hand, that also means there's no genetic base to lead us to believe that heterosexuality is genetically determined, either.

2. Neurohormonal Factors: We know hormones are responsible for determining the onset of puberty and the sexual maturation of a teenager. We know hormones control our sexual urges and drives. We also know hormones regulate our reproductive cycles and trigger the sexual development of a fetus. Neurohormonal theories hold to a cause-and-effect relationship between hormonal factors and homosexuality. For example, studies have been done to measure, analyze, and quantify the hormonal regulation of the hypothalamus (a key part of the brain that coordinates the functions of the nervous system and pituitary gland) in gay and heterosexual individuals. While these studies found some differences between gay and straight men's hypothalami, no differences could be found between gay and straight women, rendering these studies as inconclusive. Researchers have found there are too many variables to reach conclusive evidence.

Other hormonal theories point to imbalances during the life span and development (particularly in utero) that masculinize the fetus. While there may be evidence that reveals more feminine traits, it's inconclusive to correlate that with sexual orientation. Sex hormones regulate and control sexual urges and drives—this is conclusive. But there's no conclusive evidence that sex hormones direct sexual drives and desires toward a specific gender.

1.4B NURTURE THEORY

The nurture theory suggests there are external factors at the onset of a child's development that can predispose a child to homosexuality. These variables can range from parenting styles to traumatic experiences. This theory stems from Freudian psychoanalytic theories that surmise that homosexuality is predisposed from unfulfilled needs, defense of pain, and skewed parental relationships, or encoded through conscious and unconscious learning. The challenge in supporting this theory is that it's difficult to gather consistent, reproducible results. For example, we can find families who use the same parenting style, but only one child among many is gay. We also see cases where boys suffer the trauma of sexual abuse and become gay, but equally many boys do not.

"Recently, I was hanging out with a (straight) male friend in a coffee shop. As we were leaving, a group of guys began harassing me about my sexual orientation. My friend intervened and told them to stop. Then they began harassing him and calling him gay. Another time when my friend and I were out, this same group of guys attacked us. This time they beat us up bad, and we were knocked unconscious. All because I'm open about being gay." — Angie, an 18-year-old lesbian from Oklahoma

While Christians in general tend to be against Freud's theories, most buy into this particular theory about homosexuality. This is because there's some evidence that leads us to believe there is a correlation of cause and effect, learned and unlearned behaviors. Reparative therapy and sexual reorientation therapies are strongly rooted in the nurture theory. And while transformational ministries and reparative therapy techniques have had success in some cases, they've had an equal, if not higher, number of failures in reorienting or keeping a sexual orientation changed. Successful cases lead us to believe that nurture theory may be true, but the inconsistencies also lead us to no conclusion.

In addition, there's no documentation that the nurture theory has ever been attempted in reverse. If reparative therapy were consistently successful in changing a homosexual to a heterosexual, then, conversely, it should be able to change someone from a heterosexual to a homosexual.

The theories of origin of sexual preference are very involved, but what I've outlined for you above is extremely oversimplified. Queer theories, social constructs, and arguments of naturalness all play into this vast and complex issue. Nature and nurture may play a role in a sexual predisposition, but there's no evidence that either one determines it. I encourage you to start researching more thoroughly the great spectrum of theories of origin. Attempt to understand the complexities and conclusions drawn by the research. Think through the issue critically. My hope is that the church and society will thoughtfully engage in dialogue about these issues.

"I've learned that harassment in schools is the norm. Kids would scream, 'Faggot!' as they saw me in the halls. But none of the teachers said a word about it and that's what scared me...I don't feel safe at my school because I'm gay." — Kevin, a 17-year-old senior

1.4C IS SEXUAL ORIENTATION A CHOICE?

Before we get into the theories, we need to correct a myth about sexual orientation. Some people mistakenly believe it's a choice. Teenagers are told they can choose whether or not to be gay. Yet scholars and medical professionals who hold to both the nurture and nature origin theories quickly dispel this belief. While sexual behavior is learned and chosen (one chooses to engage in sexual acts), sexual orientation (one's drives, desires, and urges) is *not* chosen—although orientation can be reinforced through choice.

Consider this: Why would anyone choose to be gay when—

- In the adolescent world, the bravado of being a man is to avoid the appearance of femininity and weakness and to present oneself as sexually virile through his conversations and actions. Thus, choosing to be gay means choosing to appear abnormal and suffer rejection, isolation, and ridicule from your peers. If a teenager were to choose homosexuality, then he or she would be (knowingly) choosing to fight a painful uphill battle while attempting to adopt a nondominant identity; surrounded by non- and anti-gay messages and behaviors; and experiencing negative reinforcements, pain, and rejection regarding an identity that he or she has not yet formulated.
- Teenagers realize they run the risk of being alienated from their family and friends and causing pain to themselves and their loved ones. As a result, their need for acceptance and belonging usually leads them to choose the things that make them socially acceptable—the phenomenon of peer pressure.
- The social pressure and life scripts adolescents encounter are dominantly heterosexual. In other words, teens are constantly asked if they have a significant friend (boyfriend or girlfriend of the opposite gender), romantic relationships are typically

presented as being heterosexual, and so on. What scripts mandate that sexual orientation is a choice when heterosexuality is presented as the norm throughout a child's life?

- If homosexuality is a choice, then why is no help offered to teens regarding choosing a sexual orientation? There are no materials written, courses taught, or even testimonials given about choosing a heterosexual or homosexual orientation. No heterosexual can recall a time in their pubescence when they willfully chose between being heterosexual or homosexual. Are we to believe that homosexuals are the only ones given the opportunity to choose their orientation? What are the odds?

1.5 GLBT TEENAGERS

Gay, lesbian, bisexual, and transgendered teenagers enter into a struggle of formulating an identity that runs counter to their experiences and feelings and counter to the world around them. Ministry to teenagers who are questioning their sexuality is more effective if we better understand the process they're going through. Consider the following:

GLBT teenagers begin by asking, "Why me?" The most common secret question that GLBT teens struggle through is *Why? Why am I feeling these things? Why am I different? Why is God doing this?* The first and immediate thoughts a teen has regarding non-heterosexual orientation usually aren't positive. Throughout their lives teenagers are bombarded with heterosexual scripts from their homes, churches, and society. Roles, future dreams, success, spirituality, faith formation, and quality of life are all presented with a heterosexual ideal. When teenagers encounter something different, their natural first response is that there's something wrong with them. This notion becomes the first secret struggle to reconcile. Many GLBT teens who are raised in the church plead with God to take the homosexual desires away from them. They fight to understand why a loving God would curse them with this life. The battle becomes so painful that many would rather die than be gay.

GLBT teenagers rationalize that this is a phase they're going through. Most people begin questioning their sexuality in early pubescence when their bodies start changing and sexual maturation begins. They may develop romantic feelings for a person of the same gender. Those feelings can also become sexually arousing. They may have conversations with others about these same kinds of feelings being directed toward the opposite gender and become confused. In quietness, many teens enter their teenage years believing they're going through a sexual phase that will soon pass. And because sexuality can be such a taboo topic, they often start with the assumption that—or wonder if—other teenagers of the same gender have experienced these same feelings that run so counter to acceptable norms.

"People need to see that the bullying of lesbian, bisexual, and transgendered girls takes on the form of social terrorism. Whereas gay, bisexual, and transgendered guys may experience more physical violence." — Jill, a female GLBT advocate

GLBT teenagers live in denial of their feelings, conforming to heterosexual scripts. Confusion about sexual urges is difficult enough for any teenager, but for teens who are struggling with sexual orientation, their confusion is amped a hundredfold. So teens find safety in conforming or passing (pretending to be heterosexual). (See section 1.3a.) Denial often comes in the form of hoping this is just a bad phase. Teens who come out earlier in their teenage years tend to have less support, emotional maturity, and resources to survive the trauma. Instinctually, young people conform to the norm until they can get a stronger grasp on what they're going through.

Some teenagers feel added guilt and shame because they believe they're living a lie. Some experience a form of denial by believing that if they just have heterosexual relationships, their desires will change. Many GLBT teens date members of the opposite sex and even try being sexually active, thereby "proving" they're heterosexual. The added guilt of having brought someone else into the experience and, for some, the extra weight of immorality and sexual sin can be devastating.

"When I came home from college at the end of my freshman year, I told my friends and family about my new girlfriend. My friends seemed surprised. My best friend told me later that he and all of my other friends assumed I was gay. They thought this because I never dated or talked about girls much in high school. This really hurt me." — Mark, a straight 19 year old living in Washington

It seems that churches will more easily and quickly forgive a male teen who confesses to having sex with a female than they will a GLBT teen who shares about his or her orientation. The paradox is that the male's sin in some way validates his masculinity. So a struggling gay male may feel it's better to suffer the judgment and forgiveness of the church for having sex with a girl, thus validating his masculinity, than to be labeled gay. We don't condone sexual promiscuity, but we understand if a strapping, sexually virile adolescent guy struggles and falls. But churches aren't so gracious toward females who fall—and even less forgiving of a GLBT teenager's sexual immorality. Something is wrong with this picture. We have to change our ways if we want to help kids live healthy, spiritually authentic lives.

GLBT teenagers experience a roller coaster of negative emotions. They often feel:

- *Anger:* Sometimes they feel angry with God for making them this way or allowing them to live with homosexual urges and desires or not answering their prayers and pleas for deliverance. They may feel angry with themselves because they can't control their urges, desires, and feelings. They also feel angry with others for not being more accepting and supportive of them.
- *Loneliness:* They experience bouts of isolation because they find it difficult to relate to same-gender norms. This makes them feel like misfits.
- *Depression:* Many GLBT teenagers fall into depression because they experience a hopelessness surrounding the issue. This can put teens at a higher risk for committing self-harm or even suicide.
- *Grief and Loss:* GLBT teens struggle through the grief and loss of their dreams, hopes, goals, relationships, and a future that may now be compromised by their sexual orientation. They may also feel grief over the lack of mercy, love, kindness, and graciousness they receive from God's people. The adverse effect of this is that they may also feel envious toward those they perceive to be normalized because of a heterosexual orientation.

- *Pain and Fear:* These are probably two of the most prominent emotions in the GLBT teen's struggle with sexual orientation. They fear hurting their parents, and they're afraid of being humiliated, bullied, persecuted, and victims of violence. They feel and fear the pain over being rejected, alienated, and considered inferior. They feel pain over the derogatory comments, jokes, and disgust that are voiced regarding the issue of homosexuality. And they fear there's no safe place where they can question, struggle, and find loving support. They even feel the pain of being rejected by God and the church, which gives way to fears of judgment.

- *Guilt and Shame:* It's hard for teenagers to talk about their sexuality with an adult. It's even harder to talk about their sexual behaviors. For the GLBT teenager, this fear is greatly compounded. GLBT teenagers feel incredible guilt and shame for their sexual thoughts, drives, desires, attractions, and behaviors. Church and religion add to this guilt because many people view homosexuality as the chief of all perversions and sin. This guilt and shame makes GLBT teens feel as though they must live in silence while embracing a huge secret that eats away at their souls.

- *Confusion:* GLBT teens face confusion from having to navigate the waters of sexuality alone. They're confused about the misfit status of their sexual orientation; the messages they receive about gender identity; the seemingly false claims of a church or community to be a loving and safe place; assessing who's really safe to talk to; the relationships, attractions, and connections they have with and for others; and how to formulate their faith and convictions in the midst of their struggle.

"I wouldn't call myself bisexual or gay. I'm attracted to guys and girls, but more to girls. I only let a few people know about this...I guess I'm 'selectively out.' Too many people would judge me or bully me if they knew." — Alexis, a 20-year-old living in Ohio

GLBT teenagers live in fear of being found out or trapped. There's so much pressure on teenagers to conform to strong gender scripts that it can make even heterosexual teens deny themselves. For example, guys are taught that real men don't cry. Therefore, heterosexual guys often have to mask their feelings just to get past the "real man" threshold. So a teenager's radar is on all the time assessing, clarifying, comparing, and conforming to this gender schema. Teens questioning their sexuality tend to be even more acutely aware, and at times they may go to extremes to deflect the notion that they're gay.

GLBT teenagers begin searching for answers that can bring reconciliation to their lives. Reconciliation is not rationalization. It's an ongoing, living process of repositioning something in light of competing variables that would intersect, interfere, or interact with one's worldview. Reconciliation involves more than just fulfillment of sexual urges. For example, gay teenagers must reconcile thoughts of living life without an intimate partner; face shattered dreams and longings for having children; and battle through being fake and presenting themselves as someone they aren't out of a personal desire for safety against ethics, biblical convictions, acceptable notions, and desires and beliefs regarding quality of life. In an attempt to experience reconciliation and hope on some level, teens who question their sexuality research (it's a private, nonrelational way to seek answers) by reading about others' ideas, theologies, experiences, and so on. They're searching for some sense of normalcy.

GLBT teenagers may give way to reckless rebellion. They may begin looking at life as outsiders, rejected by the mainstream with no sense of future hope. As a result, these teens begin a slow death by engaging in reckless behaviors from the abuse of illegal substances to having unprotected, promiscuous sex. (The list of possible rebellious acts is actually much longer than this and will be discussed more in the following pages.)

GLBT teenagers formulate some conclusions about their identities, desires, and attractions. These conclusions can vary from a desire to seek gender reorientation to actual gender reassignment; from living life in celibacy to living in a committed monogamous same-gender relationship; from viewing homosexuality as sin to embracing it as God's natural design for them. Some even resolve to live in the tension of working through this issue—without full resolution—all their lives. We can lovingly walk with them on their journeys even if we don't agree with their conclusions, or we can reject them and leave them abandoned and alone.

1.5A COMING OUT

While the homosexual community cautions teenagers to make sure they're well prepared before coming out, they also pressure teens to come out, believing these teens can and will live more authentically once they do so. And some people in the gay community lack compassion for those who determine not to come out. "Be gay and proud" is the mantra of homosexuals who believe freedom comes through disclosure. If teenagers' families and friends reject them after coming out, there are gay groups and organizations that seek to embrace these discarded teens. They encourage, mobilize resources, and offer safety against the risks a gay teen may face. But most often support and care is only extended if the teenager comes out or is working toward coming out.

The belief of many gays and lesbians that "life in a closet is no life at all" is built on a presumption regarding the quality of life. Many gay men and women have refused to be defined by their sexual orientation, as do many single heterosexual men and women. They live productive lives with healthy, intact identities rooted in other things.

For example, I have a single friend whom women are always trying to "fix up" with their single nieces. He often says his life is full and rich, and he doesn't feel the need or the urge to marry. He isn't defined by his sexuality or marital status. Heterosexuals often ask me (because he's my good friend), "Is he gay?" And gay people have said to me, "He's gay, honey, a real stromo."

We are more than our sexual orientation. Teens need to hear this truth. I understand that sexuality is a very big part of identity, and I'm not trying to minimize that. However, this book is more about teenagers than sexual orientation. Teens need to determine not only to whom, how, and when they should come out, but also *whether* they should come out.

The apostle Paul speaks of a secret he had. He refers to it as a "thorn in my flesh," some struggle that kept Paul in a faith connection with God. He even says he pleaded with God on multiple occasions to take it away, but God didn't (2 Corinthians 12:7-9). Many have speculated that this could have been a physical ailment, but Paul's reference to Satan's involvement leads some theologians to believe it was more spiritually rooted. Some have guessed it was guilt over his murderous persecution of the church, while others speculate that he struggled with homosexuality. No one knows. Nowhere in the Bible is Paul's private, secret issue disclosed. And there's no historical account of anyone knowing any more about Paul's issue than we do. Paul lived productively by formulating his identity in God—the One who started a good work in Paul and was faithful to complete it (Philippians 1:6). Isn't it interesting that this is the same apostle who invites us to live in great freedom through Christ?

David, a 15-year-old, emailed his youth pastor this:
"At school people always made fun of me even though they didn't know for sure. I tried to commit suicide multiple times but couldn't do it. When I hit puberty, I wasn't normal. I didn't start to like girls, but I started to like guys."

Most churches aren't safe places for teenagers to question their sexuality. It seems that help and support are only available if a teen desires to live a certain way or seek conversion from homosexuality to heterosexuality. Coming out is viewed as either confession from a contrite heart or an act of open rebellion without any middle ground.

Coming out is traumatic. The experience can range from disclosing confusion about one's feelings, desires, and thoughts to a complete resolve and open declaration regarding one's sexual orientation. Commonly, teenagers who begin to disclose their confusion or thoughts regarding their sexual orientation do so to a close friend of the opposite gender. Typically, girls are much more gracious, accepting, and understanding than guys when a friend comes out to them.

The most significant fear about coming out to a friend is confidentiality. Many close friends run in the same social circles, so it's often difficult for teenagers to keep confidentialities. If the news leaks out, other friends may ask the struggling teen questions about his or her sexual preferences. Then the teen is usually forced to deny or come out. Most struggling teens skirt the issue, but they still must try to manage and control the damage. They fear that someone in authority or someone who's hostile toward the student will find out the truth.

This may be the point when a teenager comes out to a safe adult whom they hold in confidence. Family members—more specifically, parents—aren't usually the first people teenagers talk to about their sexual orientation. Mothers are usually told before fathers, and many mothers claim to have had some suspicions about their child's same-gender attractions.

Things to Know When a Teenager Is Coming Out
- Coming out is a process. While some may say that coming out means embracing one's sexual orientation, that isn't necessarily the case. It takes a lot of courage and fortitude for a student to disclose something so personal, especially with such strong social and religious disdain.
- Students who begin conversations about their same-gender attractions are afraid of rejection, persecution, and shame. Some even face fears of eternal damnation.
- If students seek help from a GLBT group, they'll likely be coached to assess how confident and comfortable they are with their sexual orientation before coming out. They're also coached to assess to whom, when, and how they should come out.

- Students who come out need a strong support network to help them navigate the trauma that typically accompanies this task.

1.5B BULLYING AND HARASSMENT

Incidents of bullying, violence, and aggression aimed at teenagers (often referred to as "adolescent victimization") and by teenagers is on the rise. Another book in this series, *What Do I Do When Teenagers Encounter Bullying and Violence?* notes studies indicating that GLBT teens are often the primary targets for bullying and violence. In a climate where sexual orientation is becoming more openly expressed, teens who present non-heterosexual orientations or identities are more frequently becoming the targets for verbal harassment, physical threat and assault, and even violent crimes. This goes beyond the sticks-and-stones name-calling immaturity of childhood and has reached a point of critical concern.

Bullying and violence are two sides of the same coin. Victimization begins with bullying, and at some point it crosses the line or progresses into violence. This process involves an individual or group who continually create stress, fear, and terror in the life of a targeted person or group. This terror ranges from rejection, public humiliation, insults, ridicule, and joking to shoving, beating, extortion, aggravated assault, and murder. For some GLBT teenagers, the terror is so persistent and overwhelming that they resort to suicide as a means to stop the pain. Victimized teenagers see the people around them in three categories: Bullies, bullied, and bystanders. To not be proactive against bullying and violence makes an individual (or an organization like a church) a bystander who watches without concern.

In 2007, the Gay, Lesbian and Straight Education Network (GLSEN) conducted the largest and most comprehensive study to date on bullying and violence against non-heterosexual teenagers (the 2007 National School Climate Survey). Some of their findings were:[6]

- Nine out of 10 GLBT teenagers experienced harassment during the past year for their sexual orientation. Of those students, 60.8 percent felt unsafe in their schools, and about a third of those reported skipping school within the last month because of fear.
- Nine out of 10 GLBT teenagers reported being verbally abused. Half of those reported being physically harassed (shoved, tripped, and so on) and 22 percent reported being assaulted (punched, kicked, or injured with a weapon) for their sexual orientation.
- The majority of these GLBT victims didn't report the incidents of bullying and violence because they feared retribution or worse consequences, were embarrassed or ashamed of being bullied, or believed nothing would be done about their situations.
- Of GLBT students, 31.7 percent missed a class and 32.7 percent missed a day of school in the past month because they felt unsafe, compared with only 5.5 percent and 4.5 percent, respectively, of a national sample of secondary school students.
- Lambda Legal, an organization that does research regarding GLBT issues, reports that 17 percent of the GLBT teenagers surveyed reported being assaulted and are seven times more likely than other students to be threatened or assaulted with a weapon.[7] Victimized GLBT teenagers are three times more likely to carry a weapon for their own protection and five times more likely to carry a firearm.[8]

The church should be an advocate for victimized people and proactive to usher in protection, healing, and reconciliation.

However, a huge dilemma in churches becoming advocates is that most churches aren't in relationship with GLBT teenagers. Our mission of mercy has been clouded by other agendas.

1.5C AT-RISK BEHAVIORS AND CONSEQUENCES

Teenagers struggling with same-gender attractions may be in constant turmoil. They're attempting to formulate a gender identity in a world that defines gender in "hetero" contexts. For teens with a different sexual orientation, it means constant assessment of the norms and a rigorous translation of how that fits them. Everything they feel or desire is seen as being immoral by many churches and taboo in the greater society. Now compound that feeling with a healthy dose of constant fear, rejection, isolation, and no place or nobody to turn to for support regarding this great secret—and you have a recipe for disaster.

The discouragement and defeat teens face when they question their sexuality can lead them down a path of slow destruction. The trials of adolescence alone can lead kids into destructive behaviors, but add the sexual orientation piece to the puzzle and you have GLBT teenagers at greater risk.

In his book *The New Gay Teenager*, Ritch Savin-Williams paints a brighter picture, believing that the changing climate of tolerance and awareness in Western culture has paved the way for gay teens to be freer and more embracing of a postmodern sliding range of sexual orientations.[9]

Nonetheless, there are many GLBT teenagers who engage in or are forced into the following behaviors:

Run Away and Thrown Away Many times when teenagers come out to their parents, especially parents who come from a conservative Christian viewpoint, they're forced to leave home. Some parents believe their morality demands they take a stand to not allow their child to remain under their roof as long as he or she is gay. These parents either make it so difficult that the teenager has no recourse but to run away or they wait until their child is of legal age and then kick the teen out of the house. These teenagers are called "throw-away kids."

Before we vilify these parents, we must consider another dynamic. This issue is hard on parents who also carry the same confusion, pain, and anger that their teen does. The process is equally discouraging and defeating for parents. The additional dynamic that pushes a parent to the breaking point is the destructive coping alternatives that some teens resort to. Substance abuse and other at-risk behaviors give the air of rebellion. Parents aren't trained to discern these behaviors as a means of escape; instead, they personalize them as acts of deliberate defiance.

Running away or being thrown away becomes the ultimate act of rejection.

Many teens who leave home have only temporary plans. They may bounce around from friend's house to friend's house, only staying the night and eating meals in an attempt to stay safe and maintain some of the routines in their lives, like attending school or keeping their jobs. This plan preserves the outward appearance that there is no problem, but sooner or later their welcome is exhausted.

Some GLBT teenagers don't have the network of relationships that could afford them the luxury of keeping up the appearance that everything is under control. When the temporary plan begins to unravel, the cost to the runaway teen becomes higher. Lack of funds, shelter, and food makes life on the streets a more imminent threat.

Homelessness Say the word *homeless* and it conjures up images of dirty and tattered men or bag ladies pushing piles of junk in a shopping cart. Probably the last image we have is that of a teenager who walks the streets in fear, just looking to survive. The National Gay and Lesbian Task Force, in collaboration with National Coalition for the Homeless, estimates that between 20 percent and 40 percent of the estimated 1.6 million homeless people on America's streets are GLBT teenagers. That's upwards of 640,000 homeless teenagers.

About 26 percent of those teens were told they must leave home. One-third of teens who are homeless or in the care of social services left home after enduring a violent physical assault after coming out. Thus, these teens opted for the streets as safer than their homes.[10]

Teens whose homes are in rural and suburban areas have very little access to facilities, shelters, or organizations that can assist them. These teens are forced to navigate unfamiliar urban areas where they become very vulnerable. Homeless GLBT teenagers are about seven times more likely to fall victim to violent sexual crimes than their homeless heterosexual peers.[11] The National

Runaway Switchboard, an organization that serves as the federally designated national communications system for runaway and homeless youth, found that 58.7 percent of homeless GLBT teens had been sexually victimized, compared with 33.4 percent of heterosexual runaway and homeless teens.[12]

Few shelters accommodate teenagers, and even fewer know how to protect and serve GLBT teens. Transgendered teens are alienated all the more because they're assigned shelter by birth gender. The Runaway, Homeless, and Missing Children Protection Act (RHMCPA) of 2003 (now known as the Reconnecting Homeless Youth Act, or RHYA) allocated funds for homeless youth services, which included expanded facilities, transitional living programs, drop-in centers, and street outreach programs. Many GLBT specialized facilities became the recipients of these funds. At a five-year assessment of the RHMCPA, assessors believe the programs are terribly underfunded, citing that in the year following the passage of this act (2004), about 6,700 homeless teenagers were denied service because of insufficient funding.[13]

Another alternative for these teens are the shelters and facilities run by faith-based organizations. However, most of these facilities have an agenda to convert the GLBT teen from his or her homosexuality. This includes superimposing seemingly manipulative requirements on the teens (for instance, one must attend a sermon in order to eat) or verbalizing their convictions and disdain regarding the immorality of homosexuality, all of which make the environment unwelcoming for the teen. In these facilities, many GLBT teens experience déjà vu of the abusive life they've escaped at home. Some faith-based organizations deny shelter to GLBT teens because their facilities are designed for same-gender housing and living. These organizations feel they would compromise their mission, morals, and greater clientele by having a GLBT teen living with straight teens.

I would speculate, judging from the climate, policy, and practices of our churches and private institutions, that these faith-based organizations are also driven by a fear of litigation should some incident occur, thereby conforming to the adage that it's better to be safe than sorry. Feeling belittled, mistreated, and devalued because of their sexual orientation or gender identity, some GLBT teens opt to play the game, complying with the requirements and enduring the abuse in order to survive.

Many other teens refuse to go along, and learn to survive on the streets instead. They find places to sleep in transitional programs, shower in public facilities like community colleges, and walk the streets in search of work and food. Techno-savvy runaways frequent computer stores and libraries where they can get online to communicate, scheme survival strategies with friends, and look for jobs. Most people wouldn't even know that these teens are homeless.

Other teens fail to be as resourceful and end up living under viaducts and suspended roadways, in parks, or on loading docks. Others may find shelter in crack or flop houses where they're exposed to a drug community and the perils that accompany it.

"I had a very close female friend all through high school. We were very close and got teased about it all the time from the other students who attended our Christian high school. I never thought of our relationship in a sexual way, and I don't think we were inappropriately close. Since college, I'd say that I'm bisexual, but I like girls a little more than guys. I don't plan to come out to my close high school friend." — Lisa, a 19 year old living in Virginia

School Dropouts The bullying, harassment, and violence GLBT teenagers experience in their schools has raised dropout rates to a critical level. Gay teenagers are 4.5 times more likely than their non-gay peers to skip classes because they feel unsafe. One-third are more likely to drop out of school entirely. That means the dropout rate among GLBT teens is three times the national average.[14] These statistics reflect the national trends that GLSEN found. Many GLBT teens had already missed classes or skipped school entirely to avoid the terror of ruthless bullies, thus making their GPA scores lower than their heterosexual peers.

The other factor that makes dropout a critical concern is the number of GLBT teens who've become homeless. Education ceases to be a priority for a teen trying to survive on the streets. Most homeless GLBT teens are forced to move to areas where they can find facilities and services that will accommodate them and into warmer climates to survive the elements. These urban organizations are almost always outside the school district the teen attended. The repercussions of lost education keep teens in a disadvantaged state.

Survival Sex Many homeless GLBT teens have dropped out of high school and can only find jobs that pay minimum wage. Many can't even get jobs because they're minors without proof of local residence. Unfortunately, some turn to prostitution as a means of generating income. The term *survival sex* refers to sex that's exchanged for basic needs (like cash, food, clothing, and shelter) or drugs and alcohol to feed addictions. Older men (called johns or sugar daddies) run businesses arranging homosexual encounters with younger male adolescent runaways or heterosexual sex with teenage lesbian girls. Brutality, violence, assault, sexual slavery, and sexually transmitted diseases often become part of survival sex. Most GLBT teens hate this practice but see it as their only means of staying alive.

Substance Abuse The pressures and turmoil GLBT teenagers feel can often lead them to use inappropriate coping behaviors. Coming out is usually accompanied by conflict at home, pain, rejection, and trauma. This turmoil may lead teens to medicate their pain. This usually starts with alcohol and can progress into recreational and hard drug use. Often this is a reflection of behaviors modeled in the home. Parents who go through trauma with their teenagers can also resort to abusing substances to alleviate their pain.

The Centers for Disease Control's *Youth Risk Behavior Survey* (1999) reported that GLBT teenagers had higher rates of drug use than their peers, including higher lifetime rates of using marijuana (70 percent versus 49 percent), cocaine (29 percent versus 9 percent), methamphetamines (30 percent versus 7 percent), and injected drugs (18 percent versus 2 percent).[15] There is no conclusive evidence that these statistics reflect national norms. However, social service workers have raised concerns about the increase in substance use and abuse among the GLBT teen population. Teens who end up on the streets are also vulnerable to drug use as a means of survival and association with an accepting drug community.

Self-Harm Another inappropriate coping behavior is self-harm, or self-mutilation. Self-harm characterizes lots of behaviors, the most common being cutting. Other forms of self-mutilation include branding (an act of scarring patterns into the flesh with hot wires), tattooing, and piercing. Some of these practices can be acceptable forms of fashion (body modification) within certain subcultures. But for a teen in emotional pain, the physical pain becomes a form of escape.

This behavior can also make statements intended to induce fear and intimidation, signal rebellion, and reflect self-abasement. The phenomenon of self-harm is complex. Teenagers inflict personal pain to feel alive or to displace the emotional pain they bear with a new, manageable physical pain. As long as the physical pain is present, they aren't thinking of the emotive stressors. This is why piercing and tattooing in excess can be a form of self-harm. In addition, the act of cutting creates a hormonal rush that tends to alleviate stress and pain. Girls tend to cut themselves more often than guys do, although guys who cut are far more destructive when they do it. In some cases teens may even cut, tattoo, or pierce their genitalia.

"When my parents confronted me, I denied I was gay because I didn't know for sure. Later, when I told my mom I was gay, she walked away without saying a word. She didn't speak to me for the rest of the evening and went to bed. I cried myself to sleep. My mom didn't talk to me the next morning, but I found out later she broke down sobbing at work." — Ian, a 16-year-old from the United Kingdom

Suicide Many people believe that being gay puts a teenager at a higher risk of suicide. While suicide attempts, ideation, and even completed suicides are high among GLBT teens, being gay isn't the risk factor. Suicide is the second-leading cause of death among adolescents—heterosexual or homosexual. In order to determine if suicide is higher among GLBT teenagers than straight teenagers, we'd have to know an accurate ratio of gay to straight teens. Once this is determined, we could formulate some statistical correlations. However, this is almost impossible to do since many GLBT teens hide or are curious about their orientation.

Random sample studies have been done to determine if suicide rates are higher among GLBT teens, but while they may raise some concerns, they don't offer any conclusive correlations. There is a common belief among mental health professionals that 30 percent of all teenage suicides are committed by GLBT teens. This simply isn't substantiated and has been discredited over and over again. There is no proof. Yet given the compounded and complex pressures GLBT teens are under, this common method of escape for all teenagers becomes more plausible for GLBT teenagers and should be a concern to youth workers.

Some studies have found that GLBT teenagers often only verbalize suicide ideation or make mild attempts. Still, the mental health community believes that GLBT teenagers are two to three times more likely to attempt suicide than their heterosexual peers.[16] Many teens would rather die than be terrorized, rejected, and/or bullied, and face the hopelessness of a situation in which they feel trapped.

1.6 UNDERSTANDING THE STRUGGLE

Matt is an adult who struggles with homosexuality. He recalls a very painful point in his adolescence when he was trying to understand what was happening to him. Exhausted, depressed, broken, and spiritually depleted, he set up a meeting with his youth pastor.

Matt arrived at his youth pastor's office and was greeted warmly and lightheartedly, as usual. It became obvious Matt was carrying a heavy burden, so the conversation cut right to the chase. Matt said he thought he was gay because he felt sexual attraction to guys. He barely made it farther than that sentence when his youth pastor interrupted him with, "That's so disgusting and gross. It's an abomination to God! I just can't understand how anyone could even think or feel that way. I just don't understand it at all!"

Matt walked out of the pastor's office feeling condemned and even more hopeless. He didn't go back to the church until some years later. After years of healing, spiritual renewal, and better-formulated convictions, Matt felt he needed to find that youth pastor and graciously confront him so forgiveness could occur. Unfortunately, the youth pastor was cold and indifferent when they met. He still maintained his rigid, condescending attitude and refused to understand Matt's plight or journey. If we want to help teens who question their sexuality, we need to be understanding of their journeys and pain. Understanding doesn't mean we abandon our convictions. Understanding means we empathetically involve ourselves in another person's life. When we listen and express genuine care, we're put into the right frame of mind to effectively minister. We begin to understand the confusion and cognitive dissonance a teenager is experiencing.

We become more aware of our tendencies to generalize, speak with insensitivity, and sometimes miss the mark. The complexity of the issue becomes real to us, and we're able to walk alongside teenagers in their pain.

1.6A IMAGINE THAT YOU ARE STRAIGHT

You probably read the title for this section and thought, *I don't have to imagine—I* am *straight!* Right. You know your drives, desires, tastes, lust, fantasies, and so on. You know the past, current, and future roles afforded you by your orientation. You've most likely lived comfortably within many of the gender scripts assigned to your sexuality and gender. Take a moment and think about that. Analyze it. Wrap your mind around it.

Now think about this: Everything you feel, think, and desire toward the opposite gender is the *same* thing that someone with a non-heterosexual orientation feels, thinks, and desires for their same gender or both genders.

Now consider this:
- Gay people aren't attracted to every member of the same gender any more than straight people are attracted to every member of the opposite gender. It's just as arrogant for you to believe you're the object of a gay person's desires as it is for members of the opposite gender to think they're the objects of your desires.
- Gay people don't want to have sex with children or teenagers any more than straight people do. Homosexuality doesn't make someone a pedophile. Pedophiles can be straight, bisexual, or gay.
- Gay people are as sexually driven as straight people. While many straight people live lives of rampant, hedonistic

promiscuity, they don't represent the heterosexual norm. The same is true for gay people. Sex isn't the only thing on the minds of gay people.

- A gay person's sexual orientation doesn't cloud his or her judgment, life skills, decisions, or ethics any more than the sexual orientation of a straight person does. Gay people are no less able to be decent, responsible, and competent because of their sexual orientation than a person with a straight orientation.
- Gay people don't choose their sexual orientation any more than straight people do.
- Gay people desire sex in the context of relationship just the same as straight people do. And while there are exceptions to this, those exceptions are represented in both gay and hetero communities.
- Gay people have dreams of having romance and intimacy throughout their life spans just as much as straight people do. As they grow older and experience life changes, their sexuality changes similarly to that of a straight person.
- Gay people desire to be the same genders they were born. In other words, gay men and women are no less men and women than straight men and women are. The only difference is the object of their attraction.

When we relate a heterosexual frame of reference to that of someone with a different orientation, it helps us gain a healthier perspective. For many of us, it's eye-opening to realize that gay and bisexual people are the same as heterosexuals in their desires for relationship and intimacy.

1.6B IMAGINE IF HETEROSEXUALITY WERE NOT THE NORM

Let's try to stretch our thinking a bit more. This exercise requires you to keep your *heterosexual* frame of reference while putting you in a homosexual context. This may be challenging to imagine, but work at it! You might feel as though the exercise is wrong or evil—well, maybe you won't go that far. But I hope you feel some level of discomfort. I trust it will help you become more empathetic and understanding. *Think about this fictional scenario:*

Imagine you're a heterosexual teenager living in a society where homosexuality is the norm—in fact, it's regarded as the natural inborn orientation. On the other hand, heterosexuality is considered unnatural. Homosexuality is deemed superior because gays don't have to procreate (heterosexuals have to procreate—yuck). Now let's give you a label—you're called an "oppo" because of your desire for the opposite sex.

You hang out with your friends. Almost all of them are gay (at least that's what you assume because nobody claims to be an "oppo"). They freely talk about how hot someone of the same gender is, who they desire to date, how far is too far, and so on. They point out attractive features of members of the same gender and ask you if you think that's hot, too. You can't relate because you're attracted to the opposite gender, but you play along.

Your friends joke around whenever they see someone reflecting non-gay norms, and they make comments such as, "Dude! That's so oppo!" or, "He's such a hetero." *You have hetero feelings, so how does that make you feel inside?*

You pretend you're gay because you don't want your parents, friends, or family to know you're attracted to the opposite gender. You don't feel gay attractions like your friends describe, and you begin to wonder when you'll feel the same way they do. But it never changes. As a matter of fact, you begin to feel stronger attractions to the opposite gender. You start to wonder if you're oppo. But you rationalize that maybe the right gay person hasn't come along yet to stir your feelings. You think this may just be a phase you're going through and that, any day now, you'll snap out of it. But that doesn't happen. *How does this inner turmoil affect you?*

Prom comes along and all your friends are making arrangements for the big night. You find out that a member of the same gender likes you and would love to be your prom date. Your friends pressure you to see if they can arrange something. You don't feel any attraction for this person, but now it feels like there's more pressure to keep your secret. You have to either come up with an alternative plan or fall victim to the pressure. *What will you do?*

You get invited to an overnight party. It's only acceptable to overnight with the opposite gender in your culture. And this is a problem—you're attracted to the friend who invited you to the overnight! You've been spending time with this opposite-gender friend and recently began feeling an attraction. All your gay friends have close friendships with members of the opposite gender, and they aren't the least bit attracted to them. They enjoy the relationships and do lots of things together. *What dilemma do you face in this situation?*

You feel like you're living with a secret, dodging bullets all the time. You need answers, so you search the Internet. You find all kinds of theories, theologies, ideas that present arguments, and facts—all of which contradict each other. You're sick of the arguments; you want resolve, normalcy, and spiritual wholeness. *Where will you find it?*

You decide to tell your close, opposite-gendered friend that you're an oppo and you have a heterosexual crush on him or her. You have no idea how that friend is going to respond. You fear rejection and a broken or changed friendship that keeps you distant; you fear being shamed and exposed. Your friend seems understanding at first but later leaks it that you're a struggling oppo. Your gay friends start to do one of two things: They ask you questions about your orientation all the time or they avoid you. *How are you feeling?*

All attitudes, assumptions, beliefs, and biases are gay, and you're oppo. So you have to constantly wade through the grid of assumption, translate, and carry on. *What does this do to your thinking?*

Television and movies only portray gay family situations. You struggle to understand how you're going to make it by being the square peg attempting to fit into the round hole. *How does this shape your outlook on the future?*

The expectation for success is that you'll grow up, get a good education, meet a sweet member of the same sex and get married. But you'll never meet someone of the same gender because you're not attracted to that person. So the equation gets skewed immediately. You hear talk about family and know that can't even fit into your frame of reference or the context in which you live. You just know that a gay family is the natural and only way a family can be defined. *How does that make you feel about yourself?*

You become afraid that word of your heterosexual desires is going to get back to your gay parents, so you struggle through the turmoil of when and how to tell them. This is one of the most difficult things you'll face because you've heard of oppos getting kicked out of their homes as an act of tough love and moral stand. Your relationship with your parents is already strained just because you're a teenager and you want your independence, so you wonder if this news will only throw fuel on the fire. When you find an opportunity to disclose your secret to your parents, they're caught off guard. They don't know how to react. There is a long silence, and then it becomes emotional: Anger, confusion, grief, and pain, followed by lots of crying. *What does this response do to you?*

In the days that follow, your parents are still trying to process this news. They don't understand how you can be heterosexual when they raised you gay. They're as consumed as you were with trying to wrap their minds around this, so they unintentionally distance themselves from you, not knowing how they'll react. They have questions for which they really don't want answers. They don't know how to talk to you. You feel invisible!

Your parents decide you should go to a gay treatment program that's had some success with conversion therapies. You wonder if the counselors will even understand you because they're not oppos. You feel like a mental freak because you're being sent away to a treatment program. You feel like the only choice you have in the matter is to go defiantly or go willingly. *What do you do? What do you tell your friends, employer, or youth group?*

Concerned adults (friends of your parents) who find out about this try to give you advice. Much of the time it's not gracious advice. They believe you've wounded your parents because you're choosing to be heterosexual. They tell you to just try homosexuality and change. They don't know that you already tried that. Out of desperation you engaged in gay romance and even dabbled in gay sex in an attempt to prove to yourself that you weren't oppo. *What does this do to you? Where do your conclusions lead you?*

Imagine that you're at church and you hear that you should love oppos but hate their actions and desires. Imagine that your parents, church, and society tell gay teenagers they shouldn't hang out with oppos because they have nothing in common and there shouldn't be any fellowship with them. Then imagine that the only time gays ask you to attend church is when they're having an evangelism moment. They have a difficult time with an oppo being there regularly because they really can't be your friends. *What conclusions would you draw?*

You go to your youth pastor and want to talk about why this is happening because you can't talk to your parents about it. You want someone to listen to your heart and the confusion that rages in you. Instead, you get a sermon, lecture, or apologetic about why you shouldn't be oppo and how wrong it is. You know this already, and it's really not what you needed to hear. *So what do you need?*

And let's say you even agree with your youth pastor, church, and parents—daily, you cry out to God and plead with him to take this away. But he doesn't. You wonder if it's better to be dead than an oppo. *So now what are your options as a heterosexual in a homosexual world? What will you have to reconcile? How will you have to live?*

"My brother came out when he was young. He contracted HIV/ AIDS from his gay partner. One time when he came home from college, he told me God had delivered him from swearing, smoking, and a strong substance addiction...but God didn't deliver him from homosexual attractions and desires. In the midst of fervent prayer, pleading, and agony, my brother couldn't understand why God didn't free him. My brother couldn't take the pain and disease that was ravaging his body, so he committed suicide." — Austin, a youth worker in California

1.6C GENDER IDENTITY DEVELOPMENT AND BEING DIFFERENT

While gender can be defined as male or female (the sex of a person), it can also be defined as the masculine or feminine traits a person exhibits. Gender traits are encoded through learning over a life span, but there's also evidence they could be part of a hormonal or genetic makeup. Gender identity is the development, understanding, and internalization of traits, roles, scripts, expectations, and behaviors of masculinity and femininity.

Teenagers are in a life stage in which the primary developmental task is identity. This begins with gender. They're trying to internalize what it means to be masculine or feminine. Throughout their lives they're bombarded with gender messages. They learn, assimilate, and conform to these scripts. When puberty strikes, with new physiology and greater cognitive abilities, they're thrown into the experience of analyzing their experiences and internal psyche against the messages they perceive. Identity is developed through the harmony and cognitive discourse that occurs throughout this life stage.

Gender confusion is when the natural traits of a teenager don't harmonize with accepted traits. That means a guy is naturally more feminine or a girl is more masculine. This doesn't mean they're gay. As a matter of fact, there are many gender nonconformists who aren't gay. On the other hand, there are many gay people who are gender-conformed. Teenagers who deviate from gender roles and scripts fall under great ridicule, just as gay teenagers do. This often causes them to align with the plight of gay friends (making them more vulnerable to ridicule and bullying) or adapt to rigid gender scripts and attack homosexuality. Because teenagers are in a phase of gender identity development, they police and defend rigid gender norms. Hence, their ridicule of anyone who defies the norm.

"I have a lot of friends, and I'm really involved in my youth group. But I still feel alone there. But I'd never tell anyone there...they're always joking and calling people that are dumb or people who are losers "gay." If only they knew it's *me* they're talking about." – James, a 17-year-old high school student from California

In some cases teenagers will believe they're gay because they don't or can't conform to gender scripts. They may also think they're gay if their experiences are labeled homosexual. For example, many kids have same-gender romantic and sexual encounters while learning and experimenting with sexuality. They may have tried kissing a member of the same sex or even experienced mutual masturbation in a same-sex relationship. These kids carry the baggage and doubt of thinking they must be gay even though their desires and attractions aren't for the same sex.

Gay teenagers are embracing of some of the gender norms and scripts, but they deviate when attraction, desires, and relationships intersect those scripts. Gay guys and girls who deviate from gender norms or are gender nonconformists are often ineffectually called "femme" or "butch" by other gays. For gay teenagers, the difficulty comes with discerning gender identity against what they experience. This often leads them to feel as though they're living in denial or a lie, hiding or carrying a huge secret they cannot disclose.

Transgendered teenagers navigate more tumultuous waters of gender identity. These teens find no internal correlation between their birth sex and their inborn gender makeup. Gender scripts, roles, and traits don't conform or even fit their anatomical design. These teenagers and their parents often recall how even in early childhood they had a deep sense that they weren't the gender assigned to them by birth. Parents can point back to incidents when the child would cry because he had to wear boy clothes and had a penis, or because she had to play with dolls and didn't have a penis. These children often make bold and emphatic statements that they're *not* girls or boys as assigned. Some people write off the plight of these teenagers as an attempt to justify their homosexuality.

Consider this: If there's a physiological link to gender encoding and we see gender anomalies in other areas and species of creation, is it possible that a boy can be born in a girl's body or a girl can be born in a boy's body? While we may not understand it, we have to acknowledge the possibilities. Creative design shows us that a fetus is developed gender-neutral until a certain point when anatomical parts turn into testicles or ovaries; prostate or uterus; penis or clitoris. There are also physiological anomalies where people have been born with both male and female reproductive organs. This should certainly be a factor in how we formulate our views of transgendered teenagers.

Let's consider some points where adolescent gender identity development intersects the sexual orientation of both heterosexual and homosexual teenagers:

- In a society that's learned to be more gender egalitarian and tolerant, teens are more prone to be "try-sexual," meaning they'll try anything at least once to see if it fits them.
- There is more leniency for girls to cross gender boundaries than for guys to do it. Girls can wear men's clothing, engage in masculine scripts in the name of liberation, and even adopt masculine traits, among other things. Given this, girls may not find the same amount of hostility associated with coming out that guys do. Girls may experience aversion from friends and loved ones who view a female's role in a sexual relationship as "childbearing." Some still measure women by their fertility and child nurturing.
- Girls receive messages that lesbian sex is a turn-on for guys. Some girls have resorted to becoming lesbian posers, even engaging in lesbian make-out sessions in front of guys in order to turn them on. This may be a new way of flirting and an inappropriate means of getting attention.
- Because male gender scripts are so rigid (marked with bravado and macho), guys continue to strive to prove they're men. If a guy doesn't date, is more affectionate, or is emotional, he may go to extremes to hide or suppress those behaviors to avoid being labeled.

1.6D GRIEF OF PARENTS

The process of coming out to a parent or family member is a very complex and traumatic event. There is no easy and quick way for parents to process the news they've just heard. It's widely accepted that parents work through a series of tasks or stages that mark this process much like a terminally ill patient or a person who's experienced the loss of a loved one. These stages may take hours, or they may take years, to work through. They don't follow a rigid order, but parents who've walked this path agree that the progression is fairly accurately described. It should also be noted that both parents might not process this news in the same way or at the same rate. This can create new tensions in the marriage and put further strain on everyone involved.

Shock The initial reaction from parents is often shock. This is traumatic news. Traumatic distress often gives way to shock. It's normal not to know how to respond or even to respond at all. Parents think they know their child the best and are shocked to find out something that's so far off their radar. The shock seems greater when their teen is conforming to gender-accepted scripts and passing as heterosexual (in other words, dating). Parents may bypass this stage if they had some inclination their child is gay. Parents never like to think their teenager is struggling with his or her sexual orientation, so they typically keep their observations and wonders at bay.

One couple told me their teen never talked about or showed interest in the opposite sex and seemed to be overly affectionate with a friend of the same sex. While that didn't make their teenager gay, it did raise their suspicions. For these parents, shock may be bypassed and there may be a feeling of validation.

Another set of parents found gay porn on their son's computer. When confronted, the teen denied he was gay, and the parents dismissed it. When their son came out to them later on, their minds rifled through the memories of that and other incidents they'd previously overlooked or chosen to ignore.

Fight-or-Flight Response Shock is an unpredictable state of suspension. Parents can enter into shock and stay there for a long time or fluctuate in and out of it. Shock also becomes the precursor to a fight-or-flight effect. The response following shock is anger. This is the response that struggling teens fear the most. Parents may take the opportunity to angrily lecture the teen theologically or be so disgusted that they lose their temper. Other parents flee or withdraw. They don't say anything and mull the whole thing over in silence. These parents may not know how to respond to their struggling teen. They may not talk to or even look at their child. This plays into the teens' worst fears of being rejected by their parents.

Denial Denial is a defense mechanism that numbs the pain, discomfort, and traumatic impact of an event. Denial can be a normal phase in our grief that moves to realization and resolve, or it can become an inappropriate coping strategy that can be very damaging. It can also range from emotional passivity to full-blown rage. Parents who face the news that their teen is questioning his or her sexuality experience a range of denial from ignoring the news, to modifying or rationalizing it away, to militantly battling it.

Here are some modes of denial:

- Passing the news off as a phase the teen will grow out of. Some parents view this as an experimental process or an association with a social cause (gay pride) that their child will pass through.

- Ignoring the fact that their teenager is a sexual being. It's hard for some parents to get a grip on the fact that their junior higher or young senior higher is becoming a sexual being with sexual urges, drives, and desires. Denial takes on the form that their teen is too naive to know and discern what sexual attraction is, let alone homosexual attraction. They may pass the news off by saying, "You don't even know what you're talking about," or "You're confused because you're still too young to even have sexual drives and urges."

"I came out to my church during my baptism when I shared my testimony of God's power in my life. The next few weeks after that, I noticed people were treating me differently. I'm not sure if they even know it, but they're making me feel rejected and alone now." — Riley, an 18-year-old living in New Zealand

- Choosing not to register the information is a slightly more extreme version of passing the news off. Parents may take a "That's nice—whatever" approach and gloss over the news as if it were never said.
- The more extreme version of the above response is a total abandonment of the news. This form of denial becomes an inappropriate coping strategy as the parent refuses to talk about homosexuality or anything associated with the issue. They end the conversation, change the subject, or meet the issue with hostility whenever it's mentioned. The person who assesses this best is the teen. You may hear students say, "I came out to my parents, and we never talked about it again," or "Every time I try to bring up the subject, my mom walks out of the room."

- Some parents rationalize the news as an adolescent act of rebellion, defiance, or revenge against the parent-teen tensions they've experienced. This parent may say, "You're just doing this to hurt me," or "If this is your way of rebelling, it's pretty disgusting."

- Finally, some parents deny in a militant way. They go into hyper-fix-it mode ranging from policing the teen's activities to seeking residential treatment. There may be a time and place for these activities, but it takes discernment and emotional control to do it without it becoming an act of denial. Parents who militantly deny hold on to a mentality that says, "As long as you are my child, you are not gay."

- The ultimate militant form of denial is total rejection. Parents experiencing this have such great difficulty handling the news that their child is questioning his or her sexuality that they reject the teenager by kicking him or her out of the home. They pass it off as if their child is now dead to them because of his or her choices. They refuse contact, conversation, or any form of reconciliation.

Guilt and Shame When a child comes out, parents often search for answers as to why this is happening and what caused it. This prompts them to take inventory and evaluate their inadequacies. Parents begin to feel guilt over things they said, mistakes they made, family struggles, parenting styles, lack of or insufficient spiritual and moral training, and traumas from which they didn't or couldn't protect their child. They may believe that something they've done drove their child to become gay. Usually teenagers will come out to friends before coming out to their parents. And parents may feel guilty they weren't the first to know, and question the quality of the relationship with their child. Shame comes as parents wonder what family members, church friends, clergy, and co-workers will think of their child and them.

Loss and Separation When teenagers reveal they're gay, parents process it in much the same way as they would a death. They run though a gamut of emotions—grief, separation, and loss. They begin coming to grips with a loss of hopes, dreams, and a sense of normalcy for their teenager. All parents want their children to enjoy a positive quality of life. Coming out threatens that quality.

There is a realization their child isn't who they thought him or her to be. Future hopes of being grandparents seem dashed. Grief and overwhelming concerns regarding what the teenager will encounter flood their minds. Fear of persecution and harassment, loneliness and depression, promiscuity and STDs causes a sense of normalcy to give way to deep sorrow. Some parents feel obligated to take a firm moral stance out of obedience to God, and they grieve as they feel they must choose between God and their child.

Personal Decision Making and Crisis of Faith Over time, some parents will work through the tension of loving their teenager and processing this experience. They may begin to read and learn more about homosexuality. They may question their theological stance. We allow our theology to inform us differently when we're in the middle of a situation. Parents may be faced with how to stand on their convictions and still be in a right, loving relationship with their child. They may experience as much rejection from the church as their teenager has, reframing their understanding of grace and reconciliation.

Trauma and the personal decisions that grow out of trauma often generate a crisis of faith. It's easy to have answers, opinions, and theological convictions on issues when they don't directly affect you. It's not as easy to do when the complexity and emotional trauma of an issue is overwhelmingly present in your life. Deviation from a theological consensus or internalized theological script is often viewed or labeled as compromise. This facilitates crisis. In some cases that deviation may not be compromise but a shift in a correct direction. Jesus often illustrated this when he encountered the Pharisees.

Acceptance or Rejection At some point there is resolution. Resolution can come in a wide range of responses, anywhere from acceptance to rejection. There really is no single way to describe how resolution looks. Some parents have come to great understanding and have experienced a quality of life with their GLBT children, ranging from agreeing to disagreeing to completely embracing and participating in their gay child's lifestyle. For others, resolution means a painful parting of the ways that requires a different form of reconciliation—not with each other, but first with God.

1.6E WHEN PARENTS COME OUT TO THEIR TEENAGERS

There isn't a lot of research regarding the effects on or consequences for teens who have gay or lesbian parents. It seems that many gay parents work hard at being loving parents and helping their children navigate the stigmas and challenges of being in a nontraditional family.

Regardless of how nurturing the environment, it's very difficult for a teen to process the coming out of a gay or lesbian parent. Teenagers will most likely work through the same process and stages a parent does, as mentioned in the previous section. But here are some things to be aware of:

Teens often feel betrayed and disillusioned. They attempt to juxtapose the morals they've been taught against the hidden secret the parent carried. Betrayal is also felt on behalf of the other parent. Teenagers believe they have a justified rage and may engage in risky behaviors as a result.

Teens may show disgust. Teenagers don't like hearing about a parent's sex life to begin with. Add dynamics outside their perceived norm, and a teen's disgust is even greater.

Many times the news is combined with greater trauma. The coming out announcement may be accompanied by additional news of a separation, divorce, and/or disintegration of the family. While teens have a difficult time coping with that type of news alone, the additional revelation of a parent's homosexuality compounds it.

Teens may fear shame and humiliation at their church, school, and with their friends. Fear of people finding out and a hypersensitivity to belonging (or not) can also lead the teen to act out.

Teens may wonder about their own sexual orientation. Much of a teenager's identity has been enmeshed in and drawn from the family context. When a teen's picture of the family is shattered, it may cause him or her to begin questioning and exploring issues of gender and sexuality. Some of these teens hear of or discover pro-gay evidences and genetic studies that can cause more confusion and anxiety. These teens naturally begin to wonder if they'll become (or are) gay because one of their parents is.

Difficulty accepting the parent's lifestyle. The dynamic of seeing a parent with a different partner is difficult enough for a teen. Add to this change a same-sex partner and an unfamiliar lifestyle, and the paradigm shift may be irreconcilable for the teenager. It's beyond the ability of most teenagers to make such a drastic change in perspective and expectations.

1.7 AIDS/HIV

According to the Centers for Disease Control, more than 40,000 young people in the United States have contracted AIDS since its epidemic outbreak, and about one-fourth of those have died from the virus.[17] AIDS/HIV is a growing concern with at-risk teenagers, especially minorities and those living in impoverished areas.

In 2003, approximately 50 percent of all HIV infections worldwide were found among adolescents between the ages of 15 and 24. That means 6,000 teens are infected daily, adding to the 12.4 million people already living with HIV/AIDS.[18]

Teenagers believe they're invincible. But HIV is a very real concern and risk for all teenagers. Students need to be made aware of the dangers of HIV/AIDS. This needs to be more than just a lecture in a health class.

Understanding How Theology Informs the Issue of Sexual Orientation

| Section 2 |

A theology of homosexuality is a hotbed of interpretation. Each opposing viewpoint claims to see the picture clearly. All views point to scriptural text supports, with those in opposition making accusations of proof-texting, faulty hermeneutics, and skewed logic. To delve into any one theological perspective only opens a can of worms we cannot resolve and that won't serve the purpose of this book. In the "Resources" section, I've listed some materials written from a theological standpoint across the spectrum. I trust you will familiarize yourself with the broad spectrum of views. However, in this section, I want to lay out some basic theological constructs that can guide us in our care for struggling teenagers.

2.1 BASIC THEOLOGICAL STARTING POINTS

Many Christians assert that the created design of human sexuality is with a man and a woman for procreative function (naturalness). This naturalness theory is built on the tenet that procreation is the reason God created genders. It also becomes selective, based on the conviction of the individual, as to what's natural and what isn't. Some Christians would then conclude that this is an authoritative picture that homosexuality is an abomination to God (unnatural). And they use the lamest statement as proof: "God created Adam and Eve, not Adam and Steve."

A significant flaw of this perspective is that it overlooks pleasure as being a part of the creative design for sexuality (as described well in the Song of Solomon). Those who are proponents of this naturalness view may often condone birth control or oral sex, and even sex for pleasure. However, these sexual practices aren't pro-creative, which reveals inconsistencies in naturalists' theories.

Many gays and lesbians, however, would say that naturalness is expressed by God creating some with homosexual orientation out of the complexity and beauty of design. This perspective interprets the passage found in Romans 1:25-27 that describes exchanging "natural sexual relations for unnatural ones" as supporting that homosexuals shouldn't try to be heterosexual. This view also seems to assume a lot. The assumption that there was and has always been a homosexual condition, even pre-dating the fall of humans in Genesis 3, is speculative and inconclusive.

Both views hold to a similar basic flaw: The assumption that natu-ralness of the human sexual condition is the starting place for righteousness. No natural lifestyle or condition is the authorita-tive starting point for the justification of the behaviors that grow out of it. We're clueless regarding our understanding of how sin stained and impaired every area of our lives. Isaiah gives us some insight by telling us that our best, righteous living is like putrid, filthy rags to God (Isaiah 64:6).

IMPORTANT THINGS TO CONSIDER WHEN FORMING A THEOLOGY

Our thinking regarding any issue must be in constant redemption. That would mandate we take a gracious stance and walk humbly with God.

We must remember that all sin is sin. We tend to make homosexuality a greater sin with stricter consequences. The sin of arrogance is just as vile as any sexual sin. People who use harsh, abusive language are listed right alongside the sexually immoral as some of those who won't enter the kingdom of God (1 Corinthians 6:9-10).

The good news is that nobody is outside the grace of God. If we believe that Jesus paid it all, then we must give up our desire to see others pay for their sins—whether we see it as a sin of bigotry or sexuality. We all struggle with the sin of superiority. Although we'd never admit to it, we believe that others' sins are far greater than ours. This is played out as the desire to see others pay or suffer the consequences for sin. Jesus paid it ALL. Our sin, individually and collectively, cost the life of God's Son. His atonement is powerful to transcend time, culture, physical barriers, and even our limited understanding.

Not all struggles are sin. One of the critical problems of the Christian community is that struggle is equated with the full embracing of sinful practices as behavior. We forget that Jesus was tempted like we are. Temptation, urges, thinking, and desires all become a part of the struggle. God invites us to reason through these struggles, and in them God reveals to us our salvation (Isaiah 1:18).

Perspectives on sexuality shouldn't be based on arguments of omission. Some Christians point out that there are no examples of healthy homosexual relationships described in the Bible. Homosexuals will point to the fact that while Jesus addressed all kinds of great sins, he never mentions homosexuality. We have to be careful to understand that just because the Bible is silent on an issue, that doesn't mean it's condemned or condoned.

We must constantly ask ourselves if we're making Scripture harmonize with our ideology or allowing it to transform our ideology. The application and interpretation of Scripture must be consistent to all areas of righteousness and unrighteousness. Generally speaking, Americans hold being right in the highest regard. We believe our lives are validated and our contributions to humanity are made because we have a correct view. We fail to see that the natural progression of this perspective is to believe that our agendas are God's agendas; our thoughts are God's thoughts; our crusades are God's crusades. But God reminds us in Scripture, "For my thoughts are not your thoughts, neither are your ways my ways" (Isaiah 55:8).

"I grew up in a Christian home, and I knew my parents were against homosexuality. I just avoided telling them I was gay. One day when I was home from college on break, my parents overheard my phone conversation with a friend. Immediately they confronted me about my sexual orientation. My dad had three Bibles out and opened to passages about sexuality. My mom just cried a lot. It was intense; my dad kept raging on and even asked me, 'Are you going to have sex with animals, too?' It was terrible."
— Katie, a 20-year-old student living in Maryland

2.2 THEOLOGY OF CONFESSION AND SANCTUARY

Confession and sanctuary are two theological concepts that must inform how we deal with struggling teenagers. Both start with unconditional love and grace that create a safe place. And it's only in a safe place young people can openly struggle without fear, judgment, and rejection, and in an authentic way before God.

Confession is when we remind teenagers of the absolution they receive because of Christ's powerful atonement. We speak powerful truth of hope and wholeness into the lives of teens. (See Matthew 16:19; 18:18, and John 20:22-23.) **Sanctuary** is a sacred, holy place to sense God's presence. This is a safe place where sinners find healing and protection. When you sit in a role of confessor to a struggling teenager, you must remember that the sacred space in which you sit is required to be safe, regardless of what the teen struggles with.

2.3 QUESTIONS THAT DEMAND THEOLOGICAL CONSIDERATION

Struggling teenagers face three major questions that demand theological consideration:

2.3A WHY IS THIS HAPPENING TO ME?

This inquiry is rooted in the universal question, "Why do bad things happen to good people?" And there are two deeper questions at the core:

The question of good and evil. At the center of this heated debate are two perspectives: One side sees homosexuality as good and a gift from God; the other sees homosexuality as bad and outside the boundaries of the biblical morality.

The question of pain and suffering. We don't understand the trials and tribulations of life and why God allows them. Teenagers look for examples in Scripture and in the church, but they may not be satisfied. It's important to bring them back to a theology of hope, healing, and reconciliation.

2.3B WHY DOESN'T GOD TAKE THIS AWAY?

I've encountered countless teenagers who struggle, including with their sexuality. A common desire is a deep, sincere passion to be free from the burden of sexual temptation. Theological implications to work through include these:

Understanding God's faithfulness in keeping promises. Teenagers can't understand that even if they ask God for something that aligns with his will, he may not deliver it.

Understanding our role to be faithful to God. We tend to measure our spiritual success by changed lives instead of being faithful to God regardless of the outcome. I've watched many teens walk away from the church because when change didn't occur, they were accused of not being truly repentant or not having an acceptable form or level of faith. As a result, the struggling teen is either pushed to make an insincere response or pushed out.

An understanding of true freedom in Christ. We must help teenagers realize that freedom doesn't mean we don't struggle. It means we can struggle without condemnation. Congruently, we

can also share the perspective that godliness isn't the abse[...]
sin but how we deal with sin.

2.3C WILL I GO TO HELL BECAUSE I'M GAY?
The theological implications that form this answer include these:

- How sufficient is redemption and the atonement of Christ? Did Jesus really pay it all?
- Is salvation contingent upon anything I do or don't do? Sometimes we question salvation when WE don't see fruit, so we lead teens to believe they aren't truly saved or are somehow outside God's salvation because of what they do or don't do. Do we really believe that works save or that salvation comes through the work of Christ alone?
- Is there any sin, issue, or experience that disqualifies one from being the recipient of God's salvation, reconciliation, love, and mercy? Examine Romans 8 for further direction on this issue.

2.4 SCRIPTURE PASSAGES TO CONSIDER
Only a few Bible passages directly address homosexuality. Romans 1:26-27 is the most referenced passage dealing with this issue. Many biblical scholars suggest that Paul, while using homosexuality as an illustration, is really speaking contextually of a deeper issue, such as idolatry.

I've included a list of verses for your reference. I didn't provide any additional perspectives on them because of their complex interpretations and varying theological viewpoints. These passages aren't as cut-and-dried as many believe them to be, nor should they be used as proof-texts to support any one view. Instead, they must be taken in context with everything, from the immediate passage in which it's described to the whole of Scripture.

- Leviticus 18:22—"Do not have sexual relations with a man as one does with a woman; that is detestable."
- Leviticus 20:13—"If a man has sexual relations with a man as one does with a woman, both of them have done what is detestable. They are to be put to death; their blood will be on their own heads."
- Romans 1:24-32—"Therefore God gave them over in the sinful desires of their hearts to sexual impurity for the degrading of their bodies with one another. They exchanged the truth about God for a lie, and worshiped and served created things rather than the Creator—who is forever praised. Amen. Because of this, God gave them over to shameful lusts. Even their women exchanged natural sexual relations for unnatural ones. In the same way the men also abandoned natural relations with women and were inflamed with lust for one another. Men committed shameful acts with other men, and received in themselves the due penalty for their error. Furthermore, just as they did not think it worthwhile to retain the knowledge of God, so God gave them over to a depraved mind, so that they do what ought not to be done. They have become filled with every kind of wickedness, evil, greed and depravity. They are full of envy, murder, strife, deceit and malice. They are gossips, slanderers, God-haters, insolent, arrogant and boastful; they invent ways of doing evil; they disobey their parents; they have no understanding, no fidelity, no love, no mercy. Although they know God's righteous decree that those who do such things deserve death, they not only continue to do these very things but also approve of those who practice them."
- 1 Corinthians 6:9-10—"Or do you not know that wrongdoers will not inherit the kingdom of God? Do not be deceived: Neither the sexually immoral nor idolaters nor adulterers nor

male prostitutes nor practicing homosexuals nor thieves nor the greedy nor drunkards nor slanderers nor swindlers will inherit the kingdom of God."

- 1 Timothy 1:9-10—"Law is not made for a righteous person, but for those who are lawless and rebellious, for the ungodly and sinners, for the unholy and profane, for those who kill their fathers or mothers, for murderers and immoral men and homosexuals and kidnappers and liars and perjurers, and whatever else is contrary to sound teaching" (NASB).

Practical Tips and Action to Take When Helping Teenagers Who Are Questioning Their Sexuality

| Section 3 |

3.1 GIVING SUPPORT TO A QUESTIONING TEEN

LISTEN

In preparation for this book, I talked with adolescents throughout the world who are struggling with their sexual orientation. The last question I asked them was, "What advice would you give a youth worker when he or she encounters a teen who is struggling?" The overwhelming, immediate response was LISTEN. Listening is a great gesture of love and acceptance. Kids in the middle of this struggle feel they have nowhere to turn. They're so fearful of rejection they remain silent. They need an adult in their lives who will listen to them. In our desire to help and "fix" the situation, we often get detoured from listening. We want to offer advice and solutions so quickly that we fail to hear the pain, confusion, and fear being expressed. It's critical we become quick to listen and slow to speak.

SHARPEN YOUR SKILLS

Become more alert to signs and signals of distress. Teenagers give many signals when they're experiencing great distress. Lovingly invite teens into conversation when you notice these things:

- Withdrawal or avoidance behaviors
- Dramatic changes in mood and temperament
- Possible signs of drug or alcohol use
- Ideation and conversation about suicide (even if the teen is joking)
- Shifts in sleeping and eating patterns
- Concern from the teen's friends or parents
- Changes in appearance—fashion, hygiene, and physique— which may indicate either personal distress or alignment with a subculture

MAKE IT SAFE

You need to declare you won't judge them. Let teenagers know that everyone struggles with issues of identity, and no person's struggle is greater than another's. Let teens know that you'll be available to help them to the best of your abilities. Remind teens that unless you believe harm will come to them, everything spoken about in your presence is confidential.

LOVE LARGE

Keep on affirming and reaffirming your love for teenagers. You can't express or show enough love to teens who already feel as though they'll be discarded, rejected, or condemned for what they're feeling or experiencing.

DON'T LECTURE

Remember that teenagers have probably done a lot of research and reading about the issue. They're probably aware of the arguments and theological views, to some extent, anyway. They don't need you to lecture them or sermonize. They need you to listen, love, and support.

TREAT THEM NORMALLY

Don't change your responses to them. Teenagers who question their sexuality often report experiencing a pulling away by friends and family after they've disclosed their struggle. You need to be aware of this. If you were affectionate, lighthearted, and/or adventurous with teens prior to having knowledge of their issues, then you should act the same way afterward. One youth pastor told me he stopped giving a struggling boy hugs because he was afraid it would confuse him. This is a terrible misunderstanding. Nothing changes.

HAVE AN OPEN DOOR POLICY

Safety means teens can talk with you about the issue whenever they need to. But an open door doesn't mean you have no boundaries. It means you're going to be welcoming and open to listening to their concerns, emotions, line of logic, and questions. Some youth workers get exhausted because they believe that issues should be cut-and-dried. They have equations regarding how something should be processed and corrected. If the teen doesn't follow through, then they close the door.

HELP TEENAGERS SEPARATE THE ISSUES

Pornography, sexual promiscuity, substance abuse, and a host of other things may encroach upon the lives of struggling teenagers. Help them see the dangers of these issues as separate from their sexual identity struggles. Remember the story about two boys in a bunk (in the first chapter of this book)? The first and separate issue that needed to be dealt with was the inappropriate sexual contact they displayed. The youth pastor needed to remind those teens that his response would be no different if a heterosexual couple were engaged in the same behavior. This is a separation of issues, and it keeps you in check from any kind of bigotry.

HELP TEENAGERS SEE THEY'RE MORE THAN JUST A SEXUAL ORIENTATION

There is a basic myth that sexual orientation defines the core of personage. It doesn't. We're defined by God and who he's making us to be. Scripture reminds us God began a good work in us and he will complete it (Philippians 1:6). In addition, help teens see that life fulfillment and relational fulfillment aren't the byproducts of sexuality. There are many gay and straight people whose lives are fulfilled apart from their sexuality. They even have deep, quality relationships outside their sexuality.

SUGGEST COUNSELING

Parents often want or require their teenagers to see a counselor when they're going through struggles. Some believe counseling can reorient teenagers, and some believe it will help teens overcome the depression and anguish that accompanies this issue. You need to be another voice that encourages teens to seek professional help—at least for help with the latter. Assure teens they aren't mentally ill. Let them know you'll be there to listen, but you aren't a therapist. Suggest that teens request that their parents see a counselor as well (or suggest this idea to the parents yourself).

GIVE GUIDANCE

At the appropriate time, you'll be asked for guidance or you'll be able to more fully discern the opportunity when your guidance is needed. When you give guidance and spiritual direction, you need to keep pushing teens into the arms of the Holy Spirit as Teacher. Otherwise, a danger is that you'll tell a teenager what he or she should think and do, thus making that teen dependent on you. Help teens explore Scripture and deepen their relationships with God apart from the issue. When you're asked about your personal convictions, share them; but also share how they've become your convictions and how you've explored these issues on your own. Assure teenagers you're still in the process of becoming spiritually mature and that your convictions constantly need to be put under the direction and control of the Holy Spirit, too.

3.2 CREATING A SAFE ENVIRONMENT

Many Christians confuse safety and protection for struggling individuals with an act of compromise. They cite examples of tough love, indicating that if a friend were walking toward a rushing train, you'd push them off the tracks. It's interesting that during Jesus' earthly ministry the only ones he "pushed off the tracks" were the ones doing the pushing. Jesus was always seen spending time with the sinners—eating, talking, loving, and meeting their needs even if it violated the religious Law. The Judge of the universe stepped into their lives and made them safe. And through that loving juxtaposition, many reoriented their lives. Graciousness, love, understanding, and patience mark a safe community.

Here are some practical tips that can help you create an environment of safety:

Verbally go on record that the youth ministry will be a safe place for students who struggle with any issue—including sexual orientation. The power of a verbal commitment is that it crafts a strong vision and direction for the group, while holding the group accountable. In the context of your commitment to make the youth ministry a safe place, name some things teens often struggle with. Kids will identify with those issues on many levels.

Confront inappropriate conversation. Help students realize that gossip, judgment, and slander are just as sinful as any other struggle people might encounter. Some of the most inappropriate behaviors perpetrated by adolescents are verbal ones. Gossip and rumors are probably the most destructive. Teenagers need to be challenged to keep confidentialities about the information they hear and know. They should learn to seek a person's permission before passing on sensitive information. Help students see they're engaging in a very destructive act otherwise. (See James 3.)

Students must also be challenged to eliminate degrading comments and jokes about homosexuality from their vernacular. Guys tease each other by calling one another a "fag," and girls make insensitive comments such as, "That's so gay." Students need to realize that when they talk this way, they make themselves unapproachable and unsafe. If their friend is struggling, he or she won't approach a person who makes derogatory comments because that friend has already declared a negative position. Students also need to know that when they make such comments as a member of a faith community, they make the entire community equally unsafe.

Another inappropriate verbal response is the expression of open disgust about homosexuality, bisexuality, or other alternatives. I've heard many people blurt out something like, "That makes me sick to my stomach!" when they hear anything about homosexuality. Such comments demonstrate a lack of tolerant understanding, devalue someone for whom Christ gave his life, minimize someone's plight, and establish the Christian community as being judgmental, feeling superior, and lacking understanding.

Confront inappropriate behaviors. Bullying and acts of alienation, isolation, and rejection rank high here. Leadership needs to monitor this by asking the struggling teenager how he or she assesses the climate.

Combat stereotyping and labeling. There are many people who believe they can discern if a person is straight or gay. They may refer to this as "gaydar" or "homo-discernment." The truth is that these people are stereotyping. Feminine or masculine identity traits evident in the opposite gender don't indicate that the person is gay or struggling with sexual orientation. Similarly, there are very masculine men and feminine women who are openly gay. And while there are many openly gay men and women who intentionally and flamboyantly advance gay stereotypes, we must realize they don't necessarily make up the norm.

Many straight teens, as well as GLBT teens, are hurt by stereotyping and labeling. And labeling isn't limited to gender identity either. Some people label a person's actions as gay. For example, if a teenager decides to remain a virgin or if he's affectionate with his friends, he may be stereotyped as gay. If our ministries are going to be loving communities, we must battle the labeling that so often occurs.

Keep confidentiality. Many youth workers haven't worked through a theology of confession, asylum, and sanctuary. This demands that the minister be protective, creating space where teens can wrestle through an issue, situation, or sin without judgment and fear of being publicly humiliated. It means a youth worker empathetically joins in the painful journey and keeps pointing teens back to a gracious, reconciling God. Keeping confidentiality means winning the place in a teenager's life where he or she can openly struggle. It means teens must know that you'll take their secrets to the grave, if such is mandated.

ENCOURAGE STUDENTS TO TAKE A PROACTIVE ROLE IN PUTTING A STOP TO BULLYING, HARASSMENT, VIOLENCE, AND AGGRESSION AIMED AT GLBT STUDENTS IN THEIR SCHOOLS.

Don't make all issues about sexual orientation. In the opening story, Pastor Scott was faced with the dilemma that two of his teenage guys were discovered in an act of passion while on a youth group retreat. Scott's immediate course of action should be to address the promiscuity, just as he would if this had involved a heterosexual couple. If there are consequences for violating that standard (not being allowed to attend the next retreat, for example), then those consequences should be followed in the same way but without humiliation and public reprimand. Second, the issue of the two boys' sexuality should be addressed in light of the fact that their actions "outed" them. Yet this still must be done in a gracious and loving way.

3.2A FOSTERING A LOVING COMMUNITY

Make LOVE the hallmark of your youth ministry. If you want this to happen, it needs to be talked about openly, modeled freely, encouraged strongly, and evaluated often. Every chance you get, you need to publicly and privately verbalize that LOVE is what we're about. Lead student discussions that challenge and assess if the ministry is really marked by that. Have students identify the barriers that keep the ministry from becoming a loving environment. Ask them to assess whether GLBT teens or other marginalized teens would see the ministry as loving. Define steps that need to be taken to make it a more loving place. Then model love—not just to lovable teens but to ALL people.

Encourage teens to build relationships with marginalized students. This is always a youth ministry risk because parents harbor great fears their teenager will be influenced and turn bad. You may have to start with a communication to the parents about how teenagers can be light in a dark world. You may need to dispel their fears and help them see that God is bigger than anything that could taint their teenagers. Then you may need to challenge the parents to model this behavior in their homes. Countless Christian families have no relationship with non-Christians. And many more aren't in relationship with Christian or non-Christian homosexuals.

Challenge teen leaders to be aware of newcomers. Give leadership and mature teens a vision to care for new people. Encourage them to be a host for the first month a new teenager comes to youth group. The host teenager should introduce the new teen to as many people as possible, include him or her in social plans and events, and even text or call the new teen during the week.

Avoid rivalries—youth group Is Switzerland (neutral). Competition is sometimes a good tool to use with teenagers, but it can't be the adventure that marks your ministry. Competition can stir a rivalry or breed loyalties that don't include others. Avoid school rivalries and avoid dividing your ministry into teams. Claim that youth ministry is neutral territory. Marginalized students always land on the outside of loyalties created by rivalry. They already feel as if they're made to be the losers, and have an aversion to anything that requires there be a winner.

3.2B SHOULD I CONFRONT A TEEN I BELIEVE IS STRUGGLING?

No! This is a dangerous and alienating move. Teenagers are struggling through the formation of a gender identity (maleness and femaleness). They're very conscious about the way they're being perceived. Your perception of their orientation or gender identity may not necessarily be an accurate read. If a teen isn't gay, then the confrontation could be painful and destructive.

Some believe that bringing the matter out into the open with a teenager gives him or her the freedom to discuss it. This tactic may work occasionally, but it's rare. The best tactic for getting people to talk about their struggles is to be a safe person. If a teenager knows you keep confidences, love unconditionally, and value him or her as much as and because the Creator does, then you'll find that that teen will open up to you.

Many youth workers have a messiah complex and need adolescents to need them. They want to rescue every teen. This often forces the confrontation and fosters the belief that asking the teen if he or she is gay opens a door. GLBT teens may not choose to disclose to you, even if you're safe. Coming out is a very difficult and complex process that can take a lifetime. A confrontation can force an unwanted conversation that ends with the teen denying his struggle.

3.3 MINISTRY TO PARENTS OF TEENS WHO ARE QUESTIONING THEIR SEXUALITY

Pastor Mike was caught off guard when Mr. and Mrs. Smith walked into his office to discuss the fact that they'd found gay porn all over their 16-year-old son's computer. These parents were in the middle of a struggle. But before they needed Pastor Mike's advice, they needed his support. The Smiths knew they had to confront their son and do so in a loving manner. So Mike knew they really weren't as interested in the what to do as much as they needed to get their hearts and souls around this issue and the ramifications of their discovery. They needed a safe place to process their feelings and be ministered to. Here are some basic directives that can guide you in ministering to parents who face having a child with same-sex attractions and desires.

3.3A SUPPORT FOR PARENTS

Listen. Parents may find it as scary to talk with you about this issue as a teenager does. They also fear the shame, guilt, and rejection that might occur. It's important that we be slow to speak and quick to listen.

Empathize. Understand the process that parents are going through and the incredible pain and grief over loss they may feel. Feel with them. Assure them you don't sit in a seat of judgment but will walk with them and their teenager through this journey. Acknowledge they'll have many questions you might not be able to answer, but assure parents you'll help them find answers or seek resolution.

Suggest counseling. Many parents want their teenager to see a counselor but don't believe they also need professional help to process this issue. Suggest they either go to counseling with their teenager or see someone who can help them navigate this issue. Remind them their need for a counselor doesn't mean they're mentally unbalanced. Help them see they're modeling something to their teenager by putting themselves in the same place where they want their teenager to be.

Remind them that this is still the same child. Their teenager is the same son or daughter they loved before they knew about his or her sexual attractions. Parents need to see that their teen is much more than just a sexual orientation—that the qualities and character traits are still intact. They also need to understand that you aren't minimizing the complexity of this issue or their experience, but you're enlarging their scope of their child. Remind them of the good qualities you see in their teenager. Challenge them to keep tapped into their love—and God's love—for their teen. And remind the parents of God's great love for *them*, too.

Help them hold on to hope in reconciliation. Bring them back to the goodness of God and the fact that God is continuously reconciling. (See Romans 8 and 2 Corinthians 5.) Remind them that reconciliation does come. We may not know when or what it looks like, but it does happen.

3.3B TIPS FOR PARENTS WHEN THEY ENGAGE THEIR TEENAGER

React. Often parents are caught off guard when their teenager comes out. The reactions of hurt, fear, and anger are natural and don't need to be masked. The aftermath of hearing unwelcome news is much more critical than the initial reaction to the news. If parents believe they reacted poorly, they must understand that this can be corrected and may not cause permanent damage.

Parents must help their gay teenager realize he or she must be as gracious with the parent's processing of the issue as the teen expects the parent to be toward him or her. If parents suspect that a teen is struggling with his or her sexual orientation before the teen comes out and if they have some concerns or concrete evidence (like finding gay porn on the computer), then they should lovingly confront their teen with the concern or evidence. Confrontation with evidence is much more compelling and concrete than with the subjectivity of a concern.

Parents should think through what their concern is, as well as why and how it became a concern. Parents must also realize the teenager may deny having same-sex attractions. This doesn't mean the teenager is lying. It may mean he or she is still trying to understand the struggle. Parents shouldn't make a big deal out of this but realize the conversation may be resumed at a later time. It's also important that parents not badger or shame their teen by forcing a confession with later conversations.

Be patient with the process. There is no "normal" when it comes to reaching a resolution about your child's sexual orientation.

Parents sometimes feel the pressure to get control over the issue in their minds first and then in their kid's life. This can only complicate the matter and build resentments on both sides.

Engage in dialogue. Parents should remind their teen he or she has had a lot of time to process this issue, but the parents have not. Parents should talk about their need to understand sexual orientation and the ramifications of the news they've just heard and help their teenager see that this isn't easy for them, either. Parents should encourage the teenager to be patient as Mom and Dad work through their thoughts, feelings, and convictions regarding this issue. They should also create some boundaries regarding where, when, and how the teen can enter into the parents' process, while realizing the parents should respect the same boundaries for the teenager.

Be honest with your feelings. The ways parents express their feelings to their teenager are more critical than the actual feelings the parents have. Parents can legitimately feel anger, pain, hatred, disgust, shame, guilt, loss, and hopelessness. But if their teen becomes the object of those feelings, then the consequences could be costly. Parents should be honest about their feelings but still affirm that their love for their child will remain.

Affirm and reaffirm your love for the teenager. Some parents believe love and immorality cannot inhabit the same space. They feel that if they're loving and engaging with their gay teenager, then they must be embracing their sexual identity. This isn't true. We forget that God engaged us in Jesus. God's love invaded our immorality every time Jesus talked or ate with sinners or let a prostitute wash his feet. Parents should be reminded they loved their child before they knew he or she was gay. They should help their teen see they're working hard to understand this issue and they don't know how long it will take. Ask for patience.

Stick to routines. Parents shouldn't ignore or avoid their teen just because they feel uncomfortable. Parents mustn't allow their teen's sexuality to cloud all other areas of life—the teen's or the parents'.

Think before you speak. Parents must realize that the things that come out of their mouths may have lifelong—possibly even eternal—consequences. Therefore, they should be sensitive about the types of questions they ask their teen. Questions about sexuality discussed between parents and teens are often awkward. But when homosexuality enters the picture, parents can often feel empowered to ask very personal and sensitive questions out of anger or other emotions.

Be careful about who you talk to. Taking other family members and friends into confidence may be a violation of the teen's confidentiality. Parents may not be aware of how the person they confide in will process the information and react in relationship to the teen.

Build the relationship with your teen. It takes a lot of courage for teens to come out to their parents. Even if the teen comes out in anger or vengeance—he or she still needs and desires a relationship with his or her parents.

3.4 MINISTRY TO A STUDENT DIAGNOSED WITH HIV/AIDS

Rarely do youth ministries encounter teenagers with HIV/AIDS. Most likely this is because (1) some teens may not know they've contracted the virus and therefore can't self-identify; (2) the incidence of HIV/AIDS isn't rising as dramatically among teenagers as it did in the past; and (3) our ministries aren't touching the lives of these teenagers. If you do encounter a teen with this terrible virus, here are a few pointers:

Be educated about the disease. There are countless myths and misnomers (even in an age of information) that can affect the quality of your care for a student. Many of these are generated by fear, so know the facts.

React in a loving and gracious way. LOVE, LOVE, LOVE! These teens feel like they're the lowest of the low, the ultimate outcasts, the lepers of modern society. Follow Jesus' example to love, touch, talk to, and care for these precious teens.

Listen. The best thing you can do is keep your mouth shut and listen to their stories, including their fears, dreams, feelings, pain, and so on.

Help them find the hope in staying as healthy as they can. The side effects of AIDS-arresting cocktails can be discouraging and sometimes painful. Help the student rejoice in the health of the present and focus on positive outcomes, not negative ones.

Grieve over loss. Empathize when the time comes. Because there is no cure for HIV, an infected person will begin to process the reality of his or her mortality. This is sobering and scary. Teens will run through the stages of grief and loss. Understand that process and walk along with them.

Maintain as normal a life as possible. Help the teen live life fully in the present and make future plans. Don't treat the teen as fragile, different, or odd. A teenager with AIDS is still a teenager!

Resources for Helping Teens Who Are Questioning Their Sexuality

| Section 4 |

4.1 RESOURCES

Because of the complexity of this issue, I felt it would be appropriate to give you resources across the spectrum of viewpoints so you can become more aware of the voices, arguments, and actions teenagers are engaging. Some of these resources, ranging from light to scholarly works, are in support of homosexuality, and others are against it.

If you read carefully, organizations and ideologies are mentioned throughout the rest of this book that can lead you to further research. (I won't mention them again in this resource list.) Most of those organizations have position statements and reproducible materials that present and interpret research, theologies, and theories. The design here is to give you a nudge and let you craft your own study.

4.1A ONLINE RESOURCES

• **Love in Action International** is a more conservative, Christian organization that believes that homosexuality is a condition that can be repaired through a series of programs ranging from residential treatment to reorientation counseling and programs that support families of GLBT individuals. The program is intense and not without controversy. http://www.loveinaction.org

• The **2007 National School Climate Survey** is a comprehensive study on the experiences of GLBT teenagers in U.S. schools. http://www.glsen.org/binary-data/GLSEN_ATTACHMENTS/file/000/001/1306-1.pdf

• The **Gay Christian Network (GCN)** is a Web site that allows GLBT Christians to grow in their relationship with Christ as they formulate their convictions regarding homosexuality. This organization represents those who hold to the belief that homosexuality is right within a loving, committed monogamous relationship. http://www.gaychristian.net

• **Crosswalk.com** offers a theological overview of a traditional, orthodox anti-homosexual theology. http://bible.crosswalk.com/Dictionaries/BakersEvangelicalDictionary/bed.cgi?number=T348

4.2 NATIONAL AND INTERNATIONAL ORGANIZATIONS

• **Ali Forney Center (AFC):** A housing center in New York City for homeless and runaway GLBT teens. Since 2002, this successful center has become a template for other housing facilities to help protect GLBT teens from the streets. On their Web site (under "Resources"), they list other shelters and facilities for GLBT teens throughout the United States. http://www.aliforneycenter.org

• **Exodus International:** This organization believes that GLBT people can be sexually reoriented. Labeled as a transformational ministry, this organization offers services throughout the world.

Exodus International describes itself as a "nonprofit, interdenominational Christian organization promoting the message of *Freedom from homosexuality through the power of Jesus Christ.*" http://www.exodus-international.org

• **National Association for Research and Therapy of Homosexuality (NARTH):** Their mission statement says, "We respect the right of all individuals to choose their own destiny. NARTH is a professional, scientific organization that offers hope to those who struggle with unwanted homosexuality. As an organization, we disseminate educational information, conduct and collect scientific research, promote effective therapeutic treatment, and provide referrals to those who seek our assistance. NARTH upholds the rights of individuals with unwanted homosexual attraction to receive effective psychological care and the right of professionals to offer that care. We welcome the participation of all individuals who will join us in the pursuit of these goals." http://www.narth.com/menus/mission.html

• **National Runaway Switchboard:** This organization serves as a federally designated national communication system for runaway and homeless youth. NRS's mission is to help keep America's runaway and at-risk youth safe and off the streets. http://www.1800runaway.org/

• **Soulforce:** A pro-gay social justice organization who take their mission and message to Christian university campuses and organizations throughout the world. Soulforce's mission statement reads, "Soulforce, guided by the spirit of truth and empowered by the principles of relentless nonviolent resistance, works to end the religious and political oppression of lesbian, gay, bisexual, trans-gender, queer, and questioning people." http://www.soulforce.org

4.3 WRITTEN RESOURCES

Books from a more pro-gay perspective:
• *Gay and Lesbian Theologies: Repetitions with Critical Difference* by Elizabeth Stuart. This book represents various pro-gay theological perspectives of homosexuality, gender identity, and queer theory.

• *The New Gay Teenager* by Ritch C. Savin-Williams. This book explores the attitudes, behaviors, perspectives, and values of gay teenagers. The data and conclusions in the book are drawn from many interviews with gay teens throughout the United States.

Books from a more moderate perspective:
• *The Church and Homosexuality: Searching for a Middle Ground* by Merton P. Strommen. This book presents views from every part of the spectrum of viewpoints in an unbiased way. Strommen brings the reader into the middle of this issue, contending that the militant pole on both the pro-gay and anti-gay sides violates the truth supported by the sciences, theology, and the gospel mandates.

• *What God Has Joined Together: The Christian Case for Gay Marriage* by David G. Myers and Letha Dawson Scanzoni. This book was written to help bridge the divide between marriage-supporting and gay-supporting people of faith by showing why both sides have important things to say.

Books from a more anti-homosexual perspective:

• *101 Frequently Asked Questions about Homosexuality* by Mike Haley, a proclaimed former homosexual and the youth and gender analyst for Focus on the Family. This book takes a very conservative Christian approach in answering questions about homosexuality.

• *Healing Homosexuality: Case Stories of Reparative Therapy* by Joseph Nicolosi. This book offers case studies demonstrating the tenets of reparative therapy in action.

• *Reparative Therapy of Male Homosexuality: A New Clinical Approach* by Joseph Nicolosi. This book offers a scholarly discussion regarding the environmental and social learning theories that inform homosexuality. Reparative therapy, a clinical intervention formulated by Nicolosi, is a conversion approach for helping homosexual men and women change their sexual orientation.

Other Books on Related Issues:

• *Teenage Girls: Exploring Issues Adolescent Girls Face and Strategies to Help Them* by Ginny Olson. An entire chapter in this book deals with homosexuality and gender identity development in the female adolescent.

• *Teenage Guys: Exploring Issues Adolescent Guys Face and Strategies to Help Them* by Steve Gerali. An entire chapter in this book deals with homosexuality and gender identity development in the male adolescent.

• *What Do I Do When Teenagers Encounter Bullying and Violence?* by Steve Gerali. This book takes a more comprehensive look at the issues of bullying, violence, and aggression.

Notes

1. Vicki L. Eaklor, "Gay and Lesbian Movement," *Dictionary of American History*, 3rd ed., Stanley I. Kutler, ed. (Farmington Hills, MI: The Gale Group Inc., 2003), *Encyclopedia.com*, http://www.encyclopedia.com/doc/1G2-3401801662.html (accessed January 10, 2010).

2. Ibid.

3. Ibid.

4. J. J. Conger, "Proceedings of the American Psychological Association, Incorporated, for the year 1974: Minutes of the annual meeting of the Council of Representatives," *American Psychologist* 30 (1975): 620-51, http://www.apa.org/about/governance/council/policy/discrimination.aspx.

5. Cornell University Law School, Legal Information Institute, Supreme Court collection, Lawrence v. Texas (02-102) 539 U.S. 558 (2003), http://www4.law.cornell.edu/supct/html/02-102.ZS.html.

6. The Gay, Lesbian and Straight Education Network (GLSEN), "The 2007 National School Climate Survey: Executive Summary," (New York: GLSEN, 2007). Available at http://www.glsen.org/binary-data/GLSEN_ATTACHMENTS/file/000/001/1306-1.pdf.

7. Lambda Legal, "Facts: Gay and Lesbian Youth in Schools," August 28, 2002, *LambdaLegal.org*, http://www.lambdalegal.org/our-work/publications/facts-backgrounds/page-31991643.html (accessed January 10, 2010).

8. Robert Garofalo, R. Cameron Wolf, Shari Kessel, Judith Palfrey, and Robert H. DuRant, "The Association Between Health Risk Behaviors and Sexual

Orientation Among a School-based Sample of Adolescents," *Pediatrics* 101, no. 5 (May 1998): 895-902.

9. Ritch C. Savin-Williams, *The New Gay Teenager* (Cambridge, MA: Harvard University Press, 2005).

10. Nicholas Ray, *Lesbian, Gay, Bisexual and Transgender Youth: An Epidemic of Homelessness*. (New York: National Gay and Lesbian Task Force Policy Institute and the National Coalition for the Homeless, 2006), http://www.thetaskforce.org/downloads/reports/reports/HomelessYouth_ExecutiveSummary.pdf.

11. National Coalition for the Homeless, "LGBTQ Homeless," June 2009, *NationalHomeless.org*, http://www.nationalhomeless.org/factsheets/lgbtq. html (accessed January 10, 2010).

12. National Runaway Switchboard (NRS), *Brochure of NRS Services, Stats, and Other Resources* (Chicago: National Runaway Switchboard), http://www.1800runaway.org/pub_mat/documents/LGBTQ.pdf.

13. Ray, *Lesbian, Gay, Bisexual and Transgender Youth: An Epidemic of Homelessness*, http://www.thetaskforce.org/downloads/reports/reports/Homeless Youth_ExecutiveSummary.pdf.

14. Lambda Legal, "Facts: Gay and Lesbian Youth in Schools," http://www.lambdalegal.org/our-work/publications/facts-backgrounds/page-31991643.html.

15. Centers for Disease Control and Prevention (CDC), "Youth Risk Behavior Surveillance—United States, 1999," *Morbidity and Mortality Weekly Report* 49 (June 9, 2000): 1-96, http://www.cdc.gov/mmwr/preview/mmwrhtml/ss4905a1.htm.

16. M. E. Eisenberg and M. D. Resnick, "Suicidality Among Gay, Lesbian and Bisexual Youth: The Role of Protective Factors," *Journal of Adolescent Health* 39, no. 5 (2006): 662-68.

17. Centers for Disease Control and Prevention (CDC), *HIV/AIDS among Youth* (Atlanta: U.S. Department of Health and Human Services, CDC; Revised August 2008). Available at http://www.cdc.gov/hiv/resources/factsheets/PDF/youth.pdf.

18. Lawrence J. D'Angelo, Cathryn Samples, Audrey Smith Rogers, Ligia Peralta, and Lawrence Friedman, *HIV Infection and AIDS in Adolescents: An Update of the position of the Society for Adolescent Medicine*, position paper in *Journal of Adolescent Health* 38 (2006): 88-91. Available at http://www.genderhealth. org/pubs/SAMPositionPaperHIV.pdf.

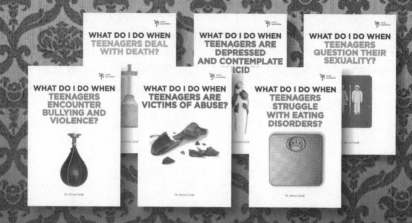

In this series of books designed for anyone connected to teenagers, Dr. Steven Gerali addresses six daunting and difficult situations that, when they do happen, often leave youth workers and parents feeling unprepared. With a background in adolescent counseling, Dr. Gerali provides valuable resources to help youth workers and parents through some of the most challenging situations they may face.

Each book defines the issue, explores how different theological perspectives can impact the situation, offers helpful, practical tips, along with credible resources to help the reader go deeper into the issues they're dealing with.

What Do I Do When Teenagers Encounter Bullying and Violence?

What Do I Do When Teenagers Deal With Death?

What Do I Do When Teenagers are Victims of Abuse?

What Do I Do When Teenagers are Depressed and Contemplate Suicide?

What Do I Do When Teenagers Struggle With Eating Disorders?

What Do I Do When Teenagers Question Their Sexuality?

Dr. Steve Gerali

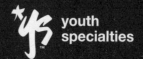

youth
specialties

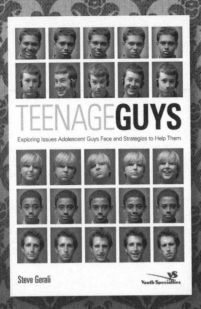

In *Teenage Guys*, author Steve Gerali breaks down the stages of development that adolescent guys go through, providing stories from his own experiences in ministry and counseling, as well as practical research findings to equip youth workers (both male and female)to more effectively minister to teenage guys. Each chapter includes advice from counselors and veteran youth workers, as well as discussion questions.

Teenage Guys
Exploring issues Adolescent Guys Face and Strategies to Help Them

Steve Gerali